HIGH YIELD

Also by Tom Berlin and Lovett H. Weems Jr.

Bearing Fruit: Ministry with Real Results
Overflow: Increase Worship Attendance & Bear More Fruit

To subscribe to the Lewis Center for Church Leadership's
free online newsletter, *Leading Ideas*, go to
www.churchleadership.com.

TOM BERLIN
LOVETT H. WEEMS JR.

HIGH YIELD

SEVEN DISCIPLINES OF THE FRUITFUL LEADER

Abingdon Press

Nashville

HIGH YIELD:
SEVEN DISCIPLINES OF THE FRUITFUL LEADER

This book is printed on acid-free paper.

Library of Congress Cataloging-in-Publication Data

Berlin, Tom.
    High Yield : seven disciplines of the fruitful leader / Tom Berlin and Lovett H. Weems, Jr.
       pages cm
    Includes bibliographical references.
       ISBN 978-1-4267-9310-3 (binding: soft back, pbk. / trade : alk. paper)   1. Christian leadership.   I. Title.
    BV652.1.B465 2014
    253—dc23

                                                                                     2014017539

14 15 16 17 18 19 20 21 22 23—10 9 8 7 6 5 4 3 2 1
MANUFACTURED IN THE UNITED STATES OF AMERICA

To
the board, president, faculty, staff, and administration of
Wesley Theological Seminary,
whose mission to equip and inspire Christian leaders
will bless the church and the world for generations

CONTENTS

LEADERSHIP
TAKES TIME

Lovett H. Weems Jr.

In each of the three books Tom and I have written together, the common theme is God's call to bear fruit. Fruitfulness is God's alternative to success. Even though it takes time for God's harvest to come, Christian leaders do their work each day with an eye toward the harvest of God's reign. In this book, we offer ways of thinking and leading that we hope will increase the yield on the planting and cultivation you do in your ministries each day. It is important to remember as we begin this journey that leadership takes time.

Will Campbell was an eccentric Baptist preacher who fought fiercely for justice but was never comfortable with the conventional practices of churches. Campbell grew up "dirt poor" in rural southwest Mississippi and was the only white person present at the formation of the Southern Christian Leadership Conference led by Martin Luther King Jr.

In 1954, a decade before the famous March on Washington, the US Supreme Court issued its *Brown v. Board of Education* decision declaring segregated public education to be unconstitutional. In the years before this decision, as the case made its way through lower courts, Campbell and some of his southern friends at Yale Divinity School lamented the fact that the decision would be made while they were away at school. Everything would be settled before they could get home to help with the transition, they thought. "Unfortunately, we were slightly off the mark," he later said.

More than fifty years after Dr. Martin Luther King's now-famous "I Have a Dream" speech, it is good to recall how change takes place—in the nation or in a congregation. Change that appears to come from isolated events—rousing speeches and mass rallies—actually is built on a foundation of leadership stretching back far into the past and with much work still to be done.

I call this "leadership lag time." There is usually a major time delay from when a concern is first addressed to when change comes to fruition. Leaders must understand this truth. If they do not, they will feel discouragement and even despair, or they will keep trying one quick-fix solution and then another. Lasting change that transforms society and congregations takes a very long time.

The modern civil rights movement in the United States provides a powerful example of this truth. During the observance of the fiftieth anniversary of D-day, C-SPAN broadcast a panel discussion that included an African American World War II veteran. One question to this panelist was whether the sacrifice by African American veterans was worth it, given the continuing racial struggles today. Without hesitation, the veteran responded, "Of course." And he quickly went on to say that most African Americans take a long view of change, knowing that any progress comes not only from the actions of a few but also from generations before who sacrificed while knowing they would never see the fruits of their labor.

Shortly thereafter, I attended our daughter's graduation at

Millsaps College in Mississippi. As the names of graduates were called, one sounded familiar—Joseph Howard Meredith. As I watched him walk across the stage, I observed that the resemblance to his father was striking. I recalled that it had taken 23,000 troops to ensure that his father, James Meredith, was enrolled in the University of Mississippi in 1962. And I remembered what the World War II veteran had said. This young man's accomplishment was built on more than his own efforts. It even went beyond the bravery of his father. It was built on the efforts of generations.

I also thought about that World War II veteran during the fortieth anniversary of the integration of Central High School in Little Rock. One of the African American students who integrated the school told an interviewer about her fear in the face of angry mobs. Finally, when additional federal troops arrived, she and the other African American students were escorted up the steps of this huge and imposing building. Then the doors opened, and they walked in. She remembers entering the school, looking all around, and saying to herself, "I am standing where none of my people have ever stood before." In that moment she knew that this giant step was based on more than her personal effort and courage. It rested on the labor of generations who never saw the rewards of their work.

Yes, as Will Campbell discovered and civil rights marchers knew well, lasting change is possible but usually not quick. However, what sustains leaders in the midst of passing victories and setbacks is the knowledge that they are a part of God's purpose. Church leaders who learn these lessons will be sustained through the inevitable challenges they will face.

Jesus said, "No one who puts a hand to the plow and looks back is fit for the kingdom of God" (Luke 9:62). Christian leaders take up the plow freely because it is the right thing to do, and they "plow in hope" (1 Corinthians 9:10) because they know that ultimately the harvest comes in God's time.

CHAPTER 1

BUILD TRUST

LOVE GOD (TOM)

There was a moment when you knew that you loved God. We are not speaking of loving the concept of God, which is where we often start in the Christian life. Parents, or the church where you grew up, may have shared the concept of God with you. Or it could have been a friend or a group you joined in college. For some time you likely drifted behind them, pulled along by their faith and experience. But there came a moment when you discovered that you loved God independent of anyone else's point of view and that brought something alive in you. Your love of God awakened a new way of seeing yourself, other people, and the world. You began to notice people whom others did not notice, and found yourself speaking to them. You began to be more careful about the words you said to others. It is possible that you started to see places where the world simply gets it wrong—the wrong values, the wrong way of treating people, and the harmful consequences of injustice to the lives of real people. And you started to care about all this in a way that gave you a new sense of purpose on some days and a new sense of weariness on others. Loving God awakens a sense of wonder in us as we see the imprint of the creator in the beauty and intricacy of the world and the people around us. That changes how we lead.

The Christian life is blessed by the incarnation, the person of God found in the person of Jesus Christ. This is why the Christian faith has a dimension that is personal. Knowing Jesus, and learning to admire and respect Jesus, changes how we think and act. Over time a deepening relationship with Christ impacts the character of the leader and also provides the focal points where your leadership gift is most clearly directed and passionately used. Jesus spoke about the importance of this relationship. He told his disciples that as God loved him, so he loved them and left them with the admonition to "abide in my love" (John 15:9).

Loving God is essential to leaders because the practice of leadership is often a solitary experience. "It's lonely at the top" is not an expression of importance. It speaks more to the nature of leadership. No matter what size the congregation you lead, there are some decisions about the present and the future that are uniquely attributed to those in leadership. When leaders work with those who follow to make changes or pursue new visions, they have to be willing to stand in front. One does not picture Moses telling the children of Israel, "You all go ahead. I'll catch up shortly." After the people celebrate crossing the Red Sea, after they place their tambourines back in their cases, Moses has to take the first steps toward the Promised Land. He and Miriam and Aaron and other recognized leaders had to step up if others were to follow.

One consequence of putting yourself forward to lead is that you have a lot of time by yourself to consider if you are headed in the right direction and what will happen to all those people behind you if it all goes wrong. It is lonely at the top, but not due to status or standing. It is lonely because that is the nature of the leader's office. While most leadership is shared with others, there is a piece of responsibility that falls uniquely to the man or woman who is ultimately accountable.

This is why being in a relationship with Christ is so powerful. Abiding in the love of Christ means that we can trust that our omnipresent God is with us and has the ability either to encourage our steps or correct our course. Because leaders are fallible, it befits us to stay in love with God. Leadership can be a consuming activity that engages the ego and sense of self-worth of those who carry the greatest sense of responsibility. What began as a God-honoring vision to serve Christ can easily degrade into activities aimed at erecting a personal monument to our efforts. Especially when critics emerge who do not affirm the plans and decisions we as leaders are carrying out, it is easy to become defensive and take everything so personally that we think far more about our reputation than serving the will of Christ.

This is why the practices that are common to those who love God are so important. Prayer, journaling, rest, solitude, worship, sharing Christian conversation, and the sacrament of Holy Communion, among other means of grace, enable us to come home to God. When we rest in our fellowship with God's Spirit, we no longer find it necessary to protect ourselves with defensive behaviors or build our self-worth through unguarded ambition.

There is nothing more important in the lives of Christian leaders than their love of God, practiced in tangible ways that keep the relationship alive over time. When God's presence is as real as our work, then God will be present in our work and will bless our gifts of leadership.

REMEMBER LEADERSHIP IS ALWAYS ABOUT A GROUP

There are many, many things about leadership that we do not know. However, there are a few truths about which we can be sure. One of the most important truths is that leadership is always about a group, not the leader. The group may be a sports team or a congregation, a youth group or a nation. The group will have a leader, but it is the group itself to which we must give attention.

That is one reason why Scott Cormode's definition of pastoral leadership is so helpful: "helping God's people take the next faithful step."[1] Leadership is not simply doing your job well, though it is better to do it well than poorly. But the performance of distinct functions does not in any way mean that the group you are leading is taking its next faithful step.

One popular model of leadership today puts the leader at the center of everything. In this view, the vision for the group comes from God to the leader, who then "casts the vision" and solicits others in its implementation. Vision is a gift of God that depends on its discovery by the leader.

A more appropriate view is to see *the group's vision* as a gift from God, given to the community. It may be first *named* by a leader or leaders. But the distinction is critical. This view assumes that God's wisdom is found throughout the community and not lodged in any one person. It also takes into account the fact that a leader often has access to more information, spends more time thinking about the visioning task, and has more opportunities than others to test out ideas in the group. Good leaders listen well, and they often can discern—rather than simply receive—God's vision.

Ronald Heifetz, who teaches public leadership at the Kennedy School at Harvard, recently said in a National Public Radio interview, "The dominant view of leadership is that the leader has the vision and the rest is a sales problem." Heifetz continued, "I think that notion of leadership is bankrupt."[2]

The inordinate focus on the leader, more so than on the group, has not always been the case. In the early development of the concept of a "professional," one of the key characteristics was that the professional is accountable to the public good. To be a professional meant to serve others rather than to be a route to personal advancement or fulfillment. The professional succeeded only to the extent that the society succeeded.

But in the church there is another step needed. While the leader's role has meaning only in relationship with the people served, so the church's leadership has no meaning apart from the wider community it serves.

One of the hallmarks of emerging views of leadership, which draw from a range of cultural traditions, is a renewed linking of leadership to the community. While he was president of Morehouse College, Robert M. Franklin asked what it might mean to have "Village Accreditation of Schools and Colleges."[3] One could just as easily ask what kind of report card our churches might receive from their surrounding communities.

Here are questions Franklin suggested might be used for such an "accreditation" (with "school" changed to "church"):

- What does the village think of the performance and value of the church?

- What has the church done in the past year to enhance the community?

- What kind of neighbor is the church?

- What could the church do to become a better citizen in its neighborhood?

These are good questions for an institution that bears the name of one who asked about water for the thirsty, food for the hungry, clothes for the naked, and release for the captives. What if our communities came to understand that our churches do indeed seek the abundant life for *all* as God's wish for them?

ATTEND TO PEOPLE IN THEIR TIMES OF NEED

If you are a leader, at some point you have probably been accused of lacking one of the following qualities: compassion, empathy, concern, or the ability to listen to others in their times of need. You may have a nagging suspicion this is true. If you have ever found yourself looking at the clock behind someone who is sharing deep sadness about the death of a great-aunt or telling about a dear son having a hard time in school and wondering if you are going to meet some deadline, it may be time to think about it.

In some places this is not perceived to be a problem. No one ever expects a wartime general to spend time asking soldiers if they are missing home. Business leaders will rarely spend time comforting workers who are negatively affected by decisions necessary for the business to survive. In both cases, these leaders may care deeply about the people with whom they serve, but direct care and compassion are not seen as necessary components of their job descriptions.

But for church leaders, this simply will not do. The problem is that the leadership gift often gives people a natural sweet spot when it comes to consideration of the big picture of vision along with the passion and ambition to achieve goals. Leaders are innately impatient to accomplish things and have a lens of personal accountability through which they examine and evaluate others. These are the exact virtues that may make caring for others difficult.

You have to think about this because you are not just a leader. You are a Christian leader. That means you are called not just "to get stuff done" but also to embody the character of Christ as you do so. That is no small task. The good news is that the qualities we so easily see in Jesus's life are now extolled in writing about leadership. It turns out that humility, compassion, empathy, and gratitude are all part of what people are looking for in great leaders.

A key to demonstrating these qualities is to care for people in their times of need. When a key donor's son needs to enter rehab, stop talking about the latest initiative and your appreciation for their financial support. Listen to what is happening, and then find ways to help. Use your network to bless them. Call them and follow up. Talk of nothing other than how their son is doing, whether progress is being made, and how it is affecting them and their family. When a staff member gets a diagnosis of cancer, find out the treatment schedule and find ways to make their burdens lighter. Visit and talk about nothing but their concerns, their health, and their experience. Speak of work only when you know it would help them to know that others are holding down the fort while they are healing. And pray. Pray with people. Pray when you are not with them because prayer both blesses the recipient and also connects us in a more personal way with those for whom we pray. If you pray for people, you are far more likely to slow down and be with them even when you are trying to keep all the plates spinning. You will keep the person in mind and be more likely to follow up when God prompts you to send the occasional note or text or make a phone call.

If you are a pastor, also make sure you and others notice and care for people who are not key leaders. When we care for people in their time of need who have no place of influence in the congregation, we show the genuineness of our love and compassion. That is when you know Christ is transforming not only your church but also you as well. The pastor does not do all the caring, of course. Many members and staff contribute to pastoral care, but a pastor staying regularly and actively involved in the joys and struggles of a cross section of the congregation can be transformative for both pastor and congregation.

There are two good reasons you should help people in their

time of need. The first is that one day you and I will meet Jesus in person, and if he thinks we just saw people as assets to be deployed instead of people to be loved, it will be uncomfortable to say the least. It is easy for leaders to begin to see people as resources rather than as children of God. This is not because you are a terrible person but because you are often pulled by the responsibilities you carry as a leader to help your church or organization take the next faithful step forward.

Attending to people in their time of need will temper this instinct. It will slow you down. It will help you find the joy Christ said would always be present when we care for others. Tom's wife, when he begins to talk about the stress of work or the demands of leadership during a particular season, has sometimes offered, "You need to go visit our members in the nursing home, I think." Her encouragement is that a helpful leadership reset is often found in the concern we show for others who may have little to offer in return.

The second reason that you want to do this is that everyone needs to know they are part of a community where all are important and mutually care for each other. Leaders should never engage in insincere acts of compassion designed to impress the people around them. However, when we model the character of Christ, when we are obedient to Christ's calling to love our neighbor as ourselves, when we visit the sick and care for the widow and orphan in their distress, it gives people who are a part of the church a sense of pride and comfort. In some ways, what the leader does for one, he or she does for all.

Christian leaders have an unusual level of connection to the needs of others. It is expected that we will show up in hospital rooms in times of sickness, be on front doorsteps at times of loss, and still help clean up after the crowd has departed the funeral reception. We live in community with one another that includes not only what happens at the time of crisis but also the months and years of conversation that follow it. The apostle Paul stated simply, "Be devoted to one another in love" (Romans 12:10a NIV). That may never make it into the leadership journals for some professions, but it is crucial for those who serve the church.

PRESUME GRACE

The gospel of Jesus Christ is a proclamation of grace. We may preach grace, but we may often function more out of judgment. As leaders, we can give to our congregations the impression that we believe we care more about the poor than they do or care more about the community, diversity, sharing the gospel, and a host of other things. That may even be true—we may actually care more. But why, in the absence of knowing the heart of everyone, would we presume the worst instead of the best? Why would our default position be to convey judgment rather than to communicate grace?

Few pastors have escaped the classic dilemma of a property committee that sets up so many restrictions on the property's use that ministry can barely take place. In frustration, it is easy to say to them, "I know you care about the bricks and mortar, but I care about people and ministry." Not good. Why would we make such an assumption? Could we not as easily assume that they care as much as we do about the people for whom those buildings were built? Imagine this alternative.

> I know that not one of you would give time to this committee if it were about bricks and mortar. The only reason you devote yourself to this task is so that when children, youth, or adults need a place for ministry, there will always be safe, well-kept, and accessible facilities for them. The whole church owes you a debt of gratitude. I'm sure you would want to know that some of our ministry leaders are having trouble making full use of our buildings. Could you name someone who might meet

with them and find out how their needs and your concerns can both be addressed?

In addition to the theological imperative for a presumption of grace, there is also a practical need. Any time we appear to devalue commitments, people cling more closely to them. They are less open to change. So if the property committee thinks their concern to prevent damage to the buildings is devalued, they will not say, "Can you ever forgive us?" They are more likely to add more locks and restrictions.

Pay attention to great leaders. You will hear them regularly use these two phrases: "I'm so proud" and "I'm so honored." Pastors should practice saying these phrases. After each should come two things: 1) something true, and 2) something you want to see more of. Practice is required because this type of language is not commonplace for many pastors.

On the Sunday following a performance by a mission college choir, the pastor said, "I was so proud of our church last Sunday because it reminded me of our longstanding commitment as a church to both music and mission." The fact is that this church still thought of itself as having strong music and mission programs; yet both had declined significantly. The pastor could just as easily have spoken from judgment. But the pastor chose to presume grace as a way of reminding them of their commitments and pointing to where they were called to go.

Clergy sometimes become anxious at this point. We might say, "When we have superb music and strong mission outreach, I will be the first to acknowledge and celebrate it." That's not how change works. Leadership is always aspirational—and especially pastoral leadership. Pastors are advocates, not news reporters of reality. We must name a vision before it is a reality. Much more work is required than graceful statements, but assuming the best is a good place to start. You point to the Promised Land before you arrive.

Assume the best until people prove you otherwise. Assume the property committee cares as much as you do about the youth who need to use the building—unless they prove you wrong. And sometimes they *will* prove you wrong. But if you are operating from a presumption of grace rather than judgment as your default way of relating to others, then you are in a much better position to say, "We need to talk. We have an issue to face." There are those times when frank discussions must take place because gaps between what the church *says* and what some *do* become pronounced. In these times, the presumption of grace pastor will be taken far more seriously than the one who leads with judgment.

Critique has its place; just make sure it is not taking *first* place.

Spend Your Own Credibility (Lovett)

Credibility is the foundation upon which all effective leadership builds. It is the "operating capital" from which leaders draw to advance the vision. At least two different types of credibility are crucial for leaders to understand and develop.

Prevenient Credibility

Those from a Wesleyan theological tradition are likely to be familiar with John Wesley's use of the concept "prevenient grace," by which Wesley referred to that basic love of God available to all people at all times. *Prevenient* means "to come before." Wesley sometimes referred to prevenient grace as the porch of true religion. However, for Wesley, prevenient grace was not the same as saving or justifying grace, which he believed would enter one's life as one grew in faithfulness.

In a similar manner, a new leader always comes with some degree of prevenient credibility. It is prevenient credibility that permits the new leader to assume responsibilities. In most cases, prevenient credibility leads to various expressions of welcome and openness to leadership changes. The degree of prevenient credibility an individual leader can assume upon arrival, however, will vary depending upon several factors.

The most recent experiences that people have had with the new leader's predecessors will help determine whether people greet that new leader with the best of assumptions or with a sense of distance and questions. Wonderful previous experiences may cause people to give you every benefit of the doubt. A disappointing experience with your predecessor may cause people to treat you with a degree of suspicion that feels uncomfortable and undeserved. In both cases, the degree of prevenient credibility afforded you has little to do with you. And even in the negative situation, prevenient credibility is not totally absent.

The degree of prevenient credibility new leaders can expect always varies, but some face special challenges. When the new leader is different from the group's cultural context (race, nationality) or different from common expectations (gender, age), then the dynamics are also likely to be different. Some of the prevenient credibility other new leaders would expect to receive may not be present in the same ways. A degree of skepticism and even resistance may be present. New leaders who are "different" are often required to "prove themselves" in ways that others are not. There is no benefit to ignoring these realities, even if they do not seem fair-minded.

Leading Credibility

Good leaders understand that they must develop their *own* credibility, not simply depend upon the credibility built up by others. Prevenient credibility may come from predecessors who have built it up through hard work. However, to use up that credibility, rather than credibility you have earned for yourself, is finally inadequate. You win your own credibility minute by minute, but you can lose it very quickly. Once lost, it may be impossible to regain.

Behavior is the key to credibility. Do people perceive us as doing what we say we are going to do? Predictability becomes a key to trust. Another source is the quality of relationships established by the leader. Therefore, the priority is to build a relationship of trust and respect with the people. Everything depends on this bonding; and helping people to address the pressing challenges they face will increase credibility and trust. Finally, and most important, there can be no trust unless the leader is trustworthy—dependable and reliable, honest and honorable. People will forgive the inevitable mistakes by a leader whom they believe to be honest, fair, and trustworthy.

Another factor contributing to credibility is for the leader to be seen as a servant of the vision of the organization. People must never doubt that your passion as a leader is directed toward what God is calling all of you as a people to be and do. Nothing devalues one's leadership more quickly than to be seen as pursuing a private agenda and *using* the church more than serving it. As a friend has put it, a leader can become a "walking credibility gap."

Being a servant of the vision and depending on credibility and persuasion more than on authority and power help make possible faithful and fruitful leadership. A leader maintains personal integrity as people see the leader's commitment to maintain the integrity of the vision. Jim Collins's concept of "Level 5" leaders describes those exemplary leaders who combine personal humility with an intense drive to accomplish the mission. It is not that these leaders do not have egos, but they channel their ambition into the organization's goals.[4]

Genuine leadership is impossible without credibility, and

credibility cannot develop without trust. These values are foundations upon which true leadership is built and grows.[5]

LEAD WHERE YOU ARE (TOM)

Picture, if you will, my daughter and me in the car together. We are in a conversation when she receives a text message on her phone. Instinctively she reads and replies with a text of her own. This goes on for five minutes. A door has opened into another world that I cannot access as I drive the car. Finally I say, "Can you do that later? *It's time to be where you are.*" Why does her texting trouble me so much?

I love my daughter. I also *like* her and enjoy time with her. Often my time in the car with her is all the time I have for uninterrupted conversation. She has older sisters, and I am painfully aware of how fast she is growing up and how soon she will be out of our home. I want to know her and be known by her, and this time is my best opportunity. It is precious.

I realize I have done something similar to the members of the churches I have served. It is easy for clergy *not to be where we are*. We are tempted to do this in two ways.

We can idealize the past. Our previous service in other churches becomes like my great-aunt Ibbie's macaroni and cheese. It was good when she served it, a favorite of our whole family, and my memory improves it every year. No one can serve me macaroni and cheese that comes anywhere close, which is not fair to the good cooks who are doing their best to offer it now.

An even more tempting option for clergy is in the other direction—dreaming of the future. An unfortunate tendency for many pastors is to live mentally and emotionally in some future place of ministry. It is easy to say, "When I get to a larger church, I will. . . . When I get to the city. . . . When I have only one church. . . . When I have a staff. . . ."

Somewhere there is a church that I picture in my imagination where I will become the pastor I believe I can be. In this church the people will respond to my preaching with deeper levels of commitments. This congregation will joyfully respond to stewardship sermons, carrying me on their shoulders and cheering as they leave the sanctuary, enthusiastic about tithing. In this church there will never be conflicts over staffing changes, strategic objectives, or renovations to the sanctuary. People will be so unified around the church's vision that decisions will be made easily by leaders and celebrated widely by the congregation.

In every church we have served, someone has left the congregation, and right before leaving they took time to make sure we knew they were leaving "because of you." In every church we have served, there have been people who ignored our preaching, identified our flaws, made promises they did not keep, confronted us over mistakes we made, and complained about things we never said nor did. It is easy, when you are a pastor, to begin to long for the sanitized past or imagine a future where what the Apostle Paul called "light and momentary troubles" (2 Corinthians 4:17 NIV) do not exist.

But as I tell my daughter when she begins texting while sitting next to me in the car, it is important to *"be where you are."* This means using the most valuable of all resources, *time*, on matters that are directly before us. Being where I am means that I patiently encourage those who are dealing with difficulty and put conflict on the table where it can be calmly considered by those involved. It means developing a thicker skin so that I do not feel devastated by what I feel are unfair criticisms and I remain tender-hearted enough to be empathetic to those who are experiencing illness or loss.

Being where you are will keep you at the leadership table during those meetings that go on longer than anyone would like because the issues are important and must be resolved if the church is going to take the next faithful step in its ministry.

Be where you are. This is the opportunity God has given you. These are people you are called to love. The church is flawed and imperfect, like the pastor. But over time, as we serve and struggle together, as we meet in times of deep compassion and care, as we celebrate our commonality and work through our differences, we can become God's people, a real community united by the love and grace of Christ.

Think about the church you would most like to serve—not by name but by characteristics. Then, get up every day determined to work toward making your current church into the one you most seek. What may happen is that over a period of years, you may serve many different churches (as the current church changes) without ever having to move.

CHAPTER 2

LEAD THE JOURNEY

NAME THE PRESENT

One of the first responsibilities of any leader is to help name the situation the group is facing. This is not the same thing as outlining your priorities or naming what you think should be done. Leaders seek to understand as objectively as possible the current context and help everyone else do the same. This is more a discovery process for a group than a describing process by the leader. If people can discover their current reality rather than depend on someone to tell them what it is, the impact on them is far more significant. Helping everyone to "get on the same page" about the current reality is essential, even if persons have differing approaches to address that reality.

Congregations can get out of touch with their true circumstances. They may not realize how out of alignment they are with the age or race or income of the surrounding community. They may not appreciate how much of the church's income is from persons already age seventy or older. The extent of deferred maintenance may be hidden. The contrast of their children's ministry with rising grade school enrollments may not be on their radar. The list can go on.

One reason to use discovery as the means of shaping an

outline of current opportunities and challenges is that the goal is always constructive. Sharing information is not to judge or reflect negatively on previous leadership. Leadership is always about building up the body of Christ. In a sense, you are asking the members of the congregation to become consultants to themselves. If they were to offer an objective report on the congregation, what might they say?

"What is the nature of the situation in which we find ourselves?" is the question you are seeking to answer. It is out of such mutual inquiry and discovery that the key elements of the current situation emerge. While many need to help discover and name this reality, the leader must keep these facts before the people in planning for the future. Such description is what spiritual leaders are called to do. Any vision of God's preferred future for a congregation will be inadequate unless it is framed within present realities. Visions emerge as God's reign and present circumstances are seen in relationship to each other. Biblical prophets, Jesus, and contemporary prophets have helped new worlds to open as people come to see the dramatic contrast between God's ways and current practices.

A leader prematurely naming the present reality may mean that the leader's interpretation of the situation remains the sole interpretation. Just saying it will not guarantee a shared consensus by those who need to be on board. It may be necessary to have long-term members with high credibility within the congregation be the ones to name particularly hard facts about finances, conflict, or unsustainable practices. Once people accept the not-so-good situation, the leader and the congregation can use that part of the church's reality to plan for the future.

Naming the present is a beginning step in leadership, but it is an important one. Be ready to be surprised by what you find. Your own prior assumptions may unravel just as much as the assumptions of longtime members. While the present state of things may be more complex and nuanced than anyone thought previously, there should emerge a limited number of major insights around which energy and planning for the future can focus. Keeping everyone focused on those big insights is a leadership task. Actively reminding people of those primary insights will go a long way toward keeping them and you from becoming distracted by lesser issues.

ENGAGE THE PAST

History is important for all congregations. It appears to be especially crucial for long-established congregations where yesterday often seems more important than tomorrow. It is not unusual for such congregations to engage in far more conversations about the glory of the past than the potential for the future. Many no longer believe the best is yet to come. What Anthony Pappas says about small membership churches is equally true for many other established congregations: "Effective small church leaders will not use bold, pie-in-the-sky visions of the New Jerusalem.... They will speak quietly about who we are on the basis of who we always have been, about how we can become even more of who we are, about what was good about the 'good old days,' and about how we can keep that good alive in our midst today."[1]

Fruitful leaders are historians who know well the ways of God and humans over the course of a congregation's heritage. It is important to understand the flow of history that brought the congregation to its current state. It helps to reflect on some key historical events in the life of the church and to understand how they have shaped and affected the congregation. Leaders find multiple ways to learn the obvious and not so obvious contours of that history. Not only will such history help explain why the church is as it is today; it will also provide much-needed material from which to draw in discerning God's new vision for the church and especially in communicating that vision in ways consistent with the church's legacy.

Learning the history is not about the past; it is about the future. You are uncovering important parts of the church's DNA and, at the same time, identifying leverage points for the future. Today's challenges may at first seem unlike anything the church has faced before until you discover stories from the past that mirror the current dilemma well. The new social issue, building program, or internal struggle is likely to trigger for the careful historian parallels that can help people put the present challenge in the light of past faithfulness. Difficult or new things may be easier once people are reminded, "That's who we are," by recalling past times. The past is filled with far more change than one might expect.

In our earlier book *Bearing Fruit: Ministry with Real Results*, Tom shared how significant his congregation's long history became in shaping a new future.[2] Tom found that the congregation's own story and values can often act as a lever that has the power to encourage members to move toward the future.

Listening to people talk about Floris United Methodist Church, Tom kept hearing a number of recurring themes:

- Make Christ the center of our lives

- A church at the center of the community

- Willing to widen the circle

- Care for others

- Serve Christ

After the themes were identified, they needed to be tested. Members confirmed they were true. They identified quickly with them and the examples Tom used to illustrate each of the themes. They could see themselves and their past in the concepts shared. A vision emerged from these themes.

Values from the past are essential to fuel energy for the future. There must be an alignment between where God is calling the church to go and at least some of its cherished values. The very process of sharing these values at Floris UMC served to educate a new generation of church members. They came to see this heritage as *their* heritage. They also shared new stories that showed that those values were alive and well. They then began to talk about their church in these terms, thereby strengthening further these commitments.

The church was embarking on some bold ventures, but everyone was confident they were building on a strong foundation. During a long-range planning session, the group spent time studying the book of Acts and talking about the church's past. At the time of the planning session, the church was in its sixth year in a new facility but already beginning to outgrow it. Sometime during that day, it was suggested that if the church were going to remain at the center of its growing community, it would have to relocate and build a third facility on a larger parcel of land that could accommodate parking and seating for those visiting the church.

It turned out that it was a senior member of the committee and a lifelong member of the church who said that as much as she liked things as they were, "When I think about our Bible study and how our church has always been open to new people in our community, I think we have no choice but to consider relocating again." That one statement captured both past and present, and it galvanized a congregation to do what it had never expected to do until they realized they had no choice if they wanted to be more of what they had always been.

Understand that the values of the past that made it such a vital time may not be visible anywhere in the present. This is why we must help congregants discover anew values from history and tell the stories of past deeds. Tom once shared this concept of the importance of the church's history with a man who was a research scientist at the National Institutes of Health. The man stopped Tom excitedly, "When you help the congregation remember their history, you are doing DNA repair. Cells do this on their own, but now we have processes that identify how a cell has been harmed, and how we can help correct the damage. The key is to understand the original state of the cell when it was healthy."

Discovering anew the values of the past is, indeed, a process of repairing a congregation's DNA and reclaiming it for the present. The church then can truly become more of what it had always been.

PAY ATTENTION TO THE CULTURE

Around the nation's capital where we both serve, there are countless policy experts. No matter what vexing issue is facing the country, these people are paid to have solutions. Normally they can provide multiple solutions. So why do problems not get solved? Why are actions not taken to address problems that cause present and long-term damage to the country? There are other people in the nation's capital who have a superb reading of where the public is on these issues, or at least the part of the public that they must face regularly for reelection. These two groups sometimes look at each other with some disdain. Policy experts know what legislation would solve the problems and so are frustrated by legislators who will not act. And politicians get frustrated with policy advisors who do not understand that every vote they make has political consequences.

The reality is that no matter how perfect the policy, in a democracy such as the United States, that policy cannot become reality unless it can "make it" in the arena of public opinion. Now, think about the church. There are those—usually including the pastoral leader—who have clear visions of God's intentions for the congregation. Whether it relates to discipleship, outreach, or the makeup of the congregation, some are particularly adept at seeing the next faithful step God has for the church. At the same time, there are others who are deeply rooted in the culture of the congregation and community and understand it well. They have a sense of what will work and what will not work. As with the nation's capital example, these people can look at each other with some suspicion. Those who see the vision feel that others are not as committed. And those who understand the culture feel that their context is being ignored. But, again, no matter how right the vision is, it can become a reality only if it can come to "swim" in the water of the culture.

Cultures are distinctive within individual churches. Even churches within a few miles of each other with almost identical demographic profiles will have different cultures. It is this distinctive DNA of a congregation that needs attention. No fruitful leader can have the attitude, "This is how I do my ministry," and then proceed to do things that way regardless of the cultural context of the congregation. A pastor brings values, but these must be held alongside the values of the congregation. Pastors may need to learn to do things that are different from their more natural preferences or inclinations because God is calling for something different in their current setting. Pastoral leadership is not about "doing one's own thing" but acting as God's servant, which requires taking a congregation's particular culture very seriously.

Needless to say, there are multiple cultures within any congregation, and the culture is constantly changing, though gradually. However, there are some cultural patterns in any congregation that separate it from others, even those nearby and composed of similar constituents. From early in their histories, churches develop their own sense of "who we are and how we do things around here," which is culture. So the vision needs to be more than right; it needs to be right "for us." Ignoring the culture can be the downfall of wonderful visions.

A relatively new pastor at a congregation knew immediately that the church had far more potential for community involvement and outreach than was currently practiced. As the pastor became aware of needs in the community, he would ask if the church had ever considered beginning a program to address those needs. The response was always the same, "We're just farmers. We can't do what other churches do." This culture was new to the pastor. The locale, attitude of the members, and approach to ministry were all different from other churches he had experienced. It would have been easy for the pastor to put such negative connotations on the local culture that fruitful leadership would have been impossible. Instead, he started viewing the vision of outreach through the lens of their culture. Soon he realized that providing food for a range of people without sufficient food was a need in the community. A vision emerged around "food for the hungry." Sure enough, those who seemed instinctively to resist new ideas spoke up: "Pastor, we can't do that. We're just farmers." Immediately the irony was evident to them and others. "Of course, we can do that. That's who we are. That's what we do. We are farmers. We feed the world."

Find ways to bring better alignment between the vision and the culture by paying attention to both.

ENVISION THE FUTURE

An extremely insightful definition of church leadership previously cited is "helping God's people take the next faithful step." But that task is easier said than done. It can come only after leaders understand history, culture, and present; a new vision emerges from these dimensions yet is also different. Fruitful leaders learn how to focus more on the continuity than the difference. As we have said, leaders find ways to frame new initiatives as "being more of what we have been" if at all possible. That means drawing from what has been selectively based on the current and future needs. It is not enough to know what is needed. Fruitful leaders find ways for the next step to be along a path and in a direction congruent with the past.

As important as continuity is, we must remember that another thing we know for sure about leadership is that it is always about change. And while, of course, we do not want change just for the sake of change, we must change because the current state of things is never synonymous with God's ultimate will. This is true for our lives, congregations, and world.

No matter how glorious the past or exciting the present, you never can say this is what God's ultimate will is. So no matter how appreciative we are of the past and present, a key role of leaders is celebrating the past and present while helping people say, "Let us turn to God and discern that next chapter and that next step."

Most churches today face challenging times. Most remember their greatest strength and presence in the community in times past. Most churches reflect the makeup of the population a few decades ago rather than today. As the population has gotten younger, more diverse, and poorer, many churches have tended to remain fairly nondiverse in their membership. Their membership has become significantly older than the general population and increasingly upper middle class. Many churches are not located where most people live today. Some have facilities that no longer fit their membership or financial capabilities. There is a long list of challenges for most congregations.

But churches also have much on which to build. All churches have tremendous assets. In many churches, there are assets not just in facilities and land but also in financial resources. Many still have a strong group of loyal members. Established churches, with all their struggles, have assets that new churches would give anything to have. These churches also are at a critical time. While aging, they still have a critical mass on which to build a new vision for the future that includes more people, younger people, and more diverse people.

There are not enough resources in most congregations to continue all that is now and "add on" a new vision. Rather, there needs to be a rethinking of the congregation's central direction. This means going back to basics. It means rethinking what is essential. It also means that we get out of a survival mode if that is where our congregation is at this time. The most important essential to reclaim is our mission. Going back to basics is the way not to survive but to thrive. We cannot devote energy to preserving God's vision for a previous era while neglecting discernment of God's new vision for our next faithful step.

All organizations, including churches, that have been around for a while must re-vision or die. Death for congregations comes not when the doors close but when God's power is no longer transforming lives and communities. That death may come decades before any formal closure. In order to thrive, churches may need a new vision to once again connect people with God and to connect with the community in which they exist.

Fruitful leadership requires the discernment of that appropriate and shared vision of what God is calling the congregation to do in the near future. The leader's role is critical in its formulation and communication. However, vision is a gift God gives to God's people and not to the leader alone. Leaders often first name the vision, even if not in its final form. Visioning is not a management exercise but a practice of spiritual discernment. We involve many people, not for political purposes but for spiritual discernment reasons. While we believe that all people have some part of the wisdom we need for the vision, we do not believe God gives all that wisdom to one person. Therefore, we find ways for the most active and inactive members to share wisdom the church needs to hear. Longtime members and newcomers bring necessary, if different, insights. It is out of careful listening, brought together with much prayer and biblical grounding, that God's vision is most likely to emerge. New visions may seem different from those of the past, but what they share with earlier visions is their power to energize an entire congregation to do what they genuinely believe to be God's will for this time and place.

UNDERSTAND HOW HARD CHANGE IS

A key challenge for pastoral leaders is to see things from the perspective of those in the congregation. Only by seeing possible changes from the perspective of the congregation's values and interests can a leader frame the proposed changes in a way consistent with that perspective and the church's culture.

Viewing change from the perspective of others permits leaders to understand better what is at stake for others, including the nature of their fears, questions, and sense of loss. A leader always tries to see things from the perspectives of those on the receiving end of change.

Change leaders anticipate the questions of others before they are asked. They understand the concerns of various groups within the congregation. They name the concerns openly and identify with the concerns of others to the extent possible.

This permits the leader to be responsive to the concerns rather than being reactive and abandoning the goals of the new vision. Leaders of change regularly ask questions of themselves as they proceed. What are the groups that have a stake or interest in the change? If I put myself in their shoes, what would I think? What questions would I have? What would I have a right to expect regarding the change process?

A computer scientist from Stanford spent a year scanning Michelangelo sculptures in Italy with a laser light. But it took the naked eye and the use of scaffolding to detect some of the most revealing aspects of Michelangelo's *David.*

Marc Levoy discovered that the two eyes of David are pointed in different directions. And the famous furrowed brow is anatomically impossible. How can one explain these seemingly unusual features? Michelangelo knew, according to Levoy, how far people would be away from the sculpture and from what direction light would be coming and, thus, designed the sculpture from the perspective of those who would view it.[3]

The sculpture was crafted based on how people would be seeing it!

So it is that fruitful leaders begin any change initiative by trying to see the proposed change from the vantage point of those who will be affected by the change. In doing so, leaders come to see quickly that the exciting new possibilities envisioned are not immediately viewed so positively by many. The problem is not in the details so much as in the idea of change itself. People often view change negatively, at least until they see that they can live with the change and, perhaps, that it may advance their values. Leaders need not think they are immune to the fear of change they do not understand or in which they have not participated. As much as clergy complain about church members resisting change, they respond in similar ways to denominational decisions they do not understand or in which they were not included.

Denham Grierson concludes that churches generally live either in the past or in the future but have difficulty living as if they could influence their own situation in the present time.[4] This is particularly true for smaller churches or churches that have struggled in recent times. It is easy for such churches to focus on maintenance rather than on transformation. Just maintaining what *is* presents enough of a challenge. And, let's be honest, for many struggling churches, change has not been a friend. Pastoral changes may have brought unwelcome variations to the worship services through the years. Political and economic changes may have had unfavorable impacts as well. Persons in such congregations often have negative feelings about change that their pastors do not understand.

Pastoral leaders must put themselves in situations where they can hear and understand the hopes and dreams, as well as the fears, of the people. Change often comes from the ideas of leaders. Leaders tend to be in virtually all the conversations leading up to changes. Change usually reflects the hopes and values of leaders. So, by the time many are first hearing about anticipated changes, leaders may be totally comfortable with what is to come. Fruitful leaders find ways to move out of this leadership bubble and find out if and why any planned change may be hard for some of the people they serve.

Believe Things Can Happen (Tom)

There was a time when it was hard for me to believe that churches could undertake major goals requiring large sums of money. I found the financial aspects intimidating. It was so bad that when I had to talk to the congregation about buying a plot of land to build a larger facility, I would mumble the amount of money it would take in a low tone. After one such lackluster performance at a church-wide meeting, the chair of the building committee pulled me aside and said, "Pastor, it doesn't matter how good the plans look or how much work we do; if you can't say three to five million dollars plainly and with enthusiasm, it's just not going to happen." I will never forget what he asked next: "Tom, do you believe this can happen? Because if you don't believe it can happen, then it simply can't."

29

One of the most important contributions a leader can make is to believe that things can happen. When we do not, they will not. It is that simple. I had to learn not only to pronounce the words, "three to five million dollars," but also to say them as though we faced a mild challenge, a shallow stream to cross, a low hurdle to jump. And before I could say the words, I had to believe them myself.

In the years since that conversation, I have been amazed at what can happen when you believe things are possible. As it turned out, the relocation and first phase of our new facility cost more than we anticipated. I had to learn to pronounce even larger numbers. And yet, it happened. Believing that it could happen and celebrating when it did led to other opportunities to exercise our faith. We have undertaken mission projects that seemed impossible, entered into community partnerships that seemed unlikely, started a nonprofit center that felt implausible, and embarked on many other adventures that started with a simple belief that they could happen.

It is not all bad when you struggle with your own lack of confidence. It will help you feel a little desperate, and that will lead you to ask others for help. Your lack of confidence will push you to assemble a solid team to lead the effort. Soon you will be asking people for other resources as well, including their time, expertise, and money. The circle will get wider and wider as you reach out to everyone in the congregation to play a part in the goal all of you are attempting to reach. Believe that things can happen because you believe in the people around you. If you can get the right people together, you will figure it out, even if the issues are complex.

It is also essential that you believe God can make things happen. There is a fine line for Christian leaders between marching people to certain failure saying, "All things are possible with God," and playing it so safe that it is evident to everyone that God need not bother to get involved. Leaders live in and with that tension. I have found that the greatest things with which I have been associated were also the sources of my greatest anxiety. If you do not lie awake every so often wondering how you got into this mess, much less how you got other people to follow you, then you probably have not entered the deepest zone of trust in God's ability to bless your efforts. It may be that the Bible's regular admonition not to worry is a response to the consistent apprehension that the people experienced while pursuing God's call. There are few, if any, biblical characters who did not fear their circumstances before they learned to stand in awe of God's power.

I have learned a great deal about trusting God from my friend Bishop John Yambasu, who leads The United Methodist Church in Sierra Leone, Africa. Sierra Leone is a country where human and financial resources are scarce. Along with its many congregations, The United Methodist Church operates schools, clinics, hospitals, camps, and children's homes, all of which stand in great need of resources. Bishop Yambasu constantly works to gather people who can lead these organizations, along with the necessary financial resources to sustain their development. Often he has to face disappointments. Doctors in his hospitals take better paying jobs in other countries. Donors are sometimes not able to fully give what they hoped to provide. Workers seek other jobs that might bring greater benefits or require less sacrifice. Add to this the difficulty of maintaining property in a tropical climate, and you have a very challenging job for a leader. I have been with him when he learned of the loss of a key employee and a significant and unexpected problem in one of his programs. He always takes things in stride. When I ask him how he handles these disappointments with such composure, he reminds me, "God is good, all the time." He speaks of God's ability to bring good out of bad and the ways that grace often is running ahead, preparing blessings we cannot yet see but will experience soon. These are not clichés to Bishop Yambasu. They arise out of a deep trust that God is able to make things happen, even when it appears that all may be lost. His faith and confidence inspire those he leads.

Sometimes it is easier to believe that things can happen because they simply must happen. Many times leaders would not choose a course of action if it could be avoided. Major initiatives come on the heels of great success that needs to be advanced, as well as great needs that must be met. Judy, the principal of the local school where Floris United Methodist Church had been a community partner for ten years, challenged us to start a four-week summer school program to replace the one the school lost when funding was cut from the budget. The school's test scores were low. Kids lost ground in reading and math over the summer. They often did not eat as regularly without school breakfast and lunch. Worst of all, gangs recruited kids who were not supervised because school was out, and their parents were working multiple lower-income jobs to make ends meet.

Key leaders met to discuss the proposal. Everyone had many questions. Where would we find enough certified teachers or the money to pay for the buses and necessary school personnel? Could we generate enough volunteers to provide classroom aides, provide breakfast and lunch, and bring special programs with music, science, and the arts? It would have been easy simply to reject the proposal based on these concerns. But the fact remained that summer school was something that the principal felt the kids needed. It was a need too great to ignore, and so Camp Hutchinson was born.

Once you believe God is able, the people around you can do great things if they do them together. And when a need is crying out for attention, you start to understand that anything is possible.

CHAPTER 3

SET HIGH STANDARDS

INSIST ON EXCELLENCE

A fast food chain ran a national advertising campaign around the slogan "What you want is what you get." They wanted to assure their customers they would actually receive what they ordered. To accomplish this, the restaurant chain instituted a double-checking system for each order. The need for this kind of campaign is emblematic of the poor quality of service and rampant mediocrity to which we have become accustomed in the drive-thru world today. This chain made a national campaign theme out of something people should expect routinely. It is sad that what should be considered ordinary service is now promoted as extraordinary.

Management writer Philip Crosby made popular the phrase "quality is free." This language reminds us that our efforts to ensure we do work right do not cost us time and money. The errors are what cost. Just think how much extra time and effort are required to correct a mistake or redo something not done properly in the first place. Spending time and implementing procedures to ensure things are done correctly may appear burdensome, but they are scarcely comparable to the cost of mistakes.

A major equipment manufacturer built a new plant. The

layout of the new plant was noteworthy in one significant way: there was no space included in the new structure for "rework," a term for products not built correctly in the first place and thus requiring rework. In the former plant the rework area had, over time, grown to be larger than the regular assembly area. What a message the new physical layout sent about a commitment to excellence.

What does this mean for fruitful church leadership? One thing it means is that people are coming to church from a society in which they routinely experience incompetence and insensitivity. Sometimes they find at church more of the same. However, this situation gives the church an opportunity to represent higher standards. In the current environment, such a commitment to excellence will certainly stand out, be noticed, and be appreciated.

While saying we "offer our best to God," do we tolerate less than the best? In the church there is often a tendency to ignore quality concerns and just do things "close to right." The irony is that in the one place where one would expect to find the highest standards for all endeavors, one may actually find more tolerance for carelessness.

Do we simply assume that much of our work will not consistently be done properly? It is distressing that people so easily suggest that to have such high standards is unrealistic. They seem to imply that no one should have such expectations. However, have you noticed how error-free payroll functions normally are? It is remarkable that an organization that can be so inconsistent in many areas will have a near perfect payroll system.

Tom and his church staff share a stated value: "better is better." The idea behind this value is that excellence honors God and best serves the church. Sadly, church is often the place where we use the phrase "it's good enough" to close out work that is unfinished or poorly performed. A great example of this is the numerous websites and books dedicated to "bulletin bloopers" found in church publications. What is required is a person who has an eye for detail to give thirty to sixty minutes a week to proofreading. Finding such a person is the one small step it would take to move toward excellence. When such a small step is seen as a huge effort, excellence will remain an elusive goal.

Over the years Lovett has been told by numerous Korean students about how their parents would go to the bank to get "new" currency so when they made their offering at worship, they truly were giving "the best" to God. When new bills were not available, on Saturday night their mothers would use a hot iron to press the older currency before it was put in the offering on Sunday. Are we offering our best to God in all that we do in our churches?

We would all do well to remember the words spoken of Jesus: "All that he does, he does well" (Mark 7:37 NEB). The church has often been a place where doing just enough to get by is sufficient. The example of Jesus should remind us of our calling to do all things well.

Avoid Control, Expect Accountability

There may have been a time when leaders could shape the future based on the authority of their office or position. That world no longer exists. Today leaders have the same responsibility for the stewardship of the groups they lead but with far less positional power to make things happen. Today's leaders must begin not with their authority or prerogatives but with the mission and vision they serve. Constituencies must be rallied to God's vision of the future with virtually no control levers. The power no longer rests with the leader but with the vision to which the leader calls for accountability. The ability of leaders to help others see the vision as a preferred future, their ability to inspire others to see all that the vision holds, and their willingness to embody the vision in their own lives and pursuits will create credibility and influence that will be far greater than any authority a title can confer.

People are often suspicious and distrusting of institutions and their leaders, which works against the credibility leaders desire to attain. People experience this distrust for good reason. Many leaders have abused the power entrusted to them. Some institutions have taken advantage of the goodwill and investment many have made in them. In response, some leaders insist that people defer to their authority, a tactic that usually causes leaders to lose power.

The surest way to lose influence is to insist on it. Those with the greatest power sometimes confuse humility with weakness and exude an air of authority that chokes loyalty and stifles the gifts of others in the organization. Just as problematic, other leaders defer so much to those around them that they enable dysfunctional people in the system while failing to provide adequate direction to the best on their team. Such leaders function as if the group is everything and there is no larger purpose or mission requiring faithfulness.

A third alternative is to see one's leadership role as helping to ensure accountability to the mission and vision—but without control. This sounds difficult. It may even seem impossible! But accountability may actually be easier since it is based now on faithfulness to mission, vision, and values, not authority. It is based on what we as a people have affirmed as our mandate. Leaders do not spend time telling people what they cannot do, but instead ask people what they are doing about the shared commitments. People will be less likely to feel the need constantly to report what they will not do because no one is telling them what they must do. Instead, everyone is busy being responsive to the shared vision because accountability is expected.

The leader may have to find new ways to engender trust with key influencers and stakeholders in the organization so that everyone can be assured that the vision is the main focus. For example, when leaders of an organization are struggling with members of their board over issues of trust and responsibility, it is time to define what some call the forty-acre fence. By asking about the boundaries of decision making, the leader demonstrates that she or he is seeking personal accountability. The forty-acre fence defines the scope of authority a leader has before he or she has to call the board for approval. Sometimes the forty-acre fence is financial. The leader has a budget. As long as the leader does not exceed the budget, she or he can reallocate funds up to a certain amount between line items. Other times the forty-acre fence is around decision making. The board empowers the leader to make decisions in certain zones of operational responsibility that are later reported to the group. By asking for the parameters of the forty-acre fence, leaders demonstrate that they understand they have positional responsibility, not unlimited personal authority. This allows the group to build greater trust and to focus again on the purpose of the organization.

The great benefit of the forty-acre fence conversation is that it puts important matters in front of leaders so they can mutually decide what authority each person has and how to serve the vision of the organization in the most faithful and fruitful manner. If these issues are not discussed, they will remain unresolved and engender distrust. The clarity that often follows these conversations helps everyone to know the boundaries of accountability and decision making. As leaders exercise their defined authority without criticism or intervention from board members, everyone begins to hold greater trust in the larger leadership team even as they exercise their unique gifts. As board members see a leader work within the agreed-upon boundaries, they feel less need to assert control over the leader. The meetings that follow are far more likely to be devoted to creative problem solving and mutual conversation about the best ways to serve the vision of the organization.

Leaders no longer shape the future of their congregations based on the authority of their office. They expect accountability to the vision developed and shared among the people. And they create conversations in which there is clarity about boundaries and accountability for everyone. Among the most powerful boundaries may be the ways we grow in faithfulness and fruitfulness as the community becomes grounded in trust.

PAY ATTENTION TO THE SMALL THINGS

In the early 1980s, a successful airline executive became president of a financially troubled international airline. Within one year under his leadership, the airline returned to profitability amid an unfavorable international travel economy. More importantly, this airline quickly became a standard within the airline industry for quality, service, and reliability.

What was the secret? There was no one secret, but a conclusion this executive reached early in his tenure proved pivotal. He decided that it was impossible for his airline to become 100 percent better than the competition but that it was realistic for them to become 1 percent better in a hundred different ways.

Effective leaders focus on the one thing most crucial, but they are also attentive to the one hundred (or one thousand) things in which modest improvement can be made. The net impact of all the many small, incremental improvements can be just as powerful over a period of time as giant breakthroughs.

A design manager for Hallmark Cards said to Lovett one day, "I always look at the corners." He pointed to the doors of the building in which they were standing and noted that when those doors were painted, the paint was not properly and accurately scraped from the corners of the glass pane in the middle of the door. "People using this building will never leave saying (or even realizing) that the paint had not been scraped from the corners of the glass," he said. "However, they will leave with an impression of the building (and the organization) that is shaped by those corners."

Think about the corners of our work that we need to watch.

Preparing for a funeral, Tom entered the sanctuary, walked down the aisle, and straightened some plants and flowers in the chancel area. He moved microphone cords so that they would be hidden. He picked up some sheet music the pianist had left behind Sunday. While he did this, he thought about the ninety-four-year-old matriarch of the church whose life would be celebrated that day. She had supported the church over years of growth, relocation, and change. She had been a voice of wisdom and encouragement to a long line of pastors. A church member gently chastised him, "Tom, you don't have to do all that. It looks fine."

Tom replied, "Well, this is Elizabeth's funeral, and after all she meant to us over the years, I just want it right."

The church member replied, "Tom, the thing about you is that you want *everything* right."

For a long time Tom was not sure how to take that statement. Perhaps he was too focused on the details. Maybe it was a sign of a controlling personality. But the truth was that he *did* want everything right. He wanted guests at the funeral to know that extra care went into the preparations for this service, that Elizabeth was considered special here, and that everyone understood and appreciated all that she had given. And he wanted the church to look right at other times as well. Few things are more telling about a congregation than a facility that appears disorganized and unloved.

You can see instantly when people pay attention to the details of the church facility. The grounds are mowed and trimmed. The paint looks clean and new. Inside the facility, floors and surfaces are clean. There are no piles of paper, books, or old equipment lying about. Classrooms do not look like storerooms. Instead, they are ready and waiting for people to use them to grow in their faith. When you encounter such a church, a statement has been made about the importance of what is happening there, whether it is worship in the sanctuary or the discipleship that is happening in spaces dedicated to children and students. Not everyone has an eye for detail. But those charged with the task of cleaning and ordering the facility must. Sometimes it helps to find people who have an eye for cleanliness and interior design to walk through occasionally to help others see where improvements could be made and to offer suggestions for how to make them in a cost-effective manner.

Likewise, it is wise for leaders to pay attention to the personal habits people have in the organization. Sitting at a freshman orientation session with his daughter, Tom heard President Paul Tribble of Christopher Newport University talk about the "speaking tradition" he has established. When students, professors, or staff pass each other on campus, it is expected that they will greet each other in some way, whether by name or by simply wishing each other a good morning or afternoon. President Tribble shared that greeting each other is an important detail of hospitality and friendliness. It also trains students for their professional life beyond college. He further demonstrated his commitment to friendliness when he invited members of the freshman class to the president's open house, which was held at his home. It is just a one-evening event over the course of four years, but it communicates volumes about the personal connection he is trying to establish.

How does the staff of your church greet each other? Do they introduce volunteers to each other so that people feel welcome and comfortable? These are the types of people-oriented details that may seem unimportant but, when attended to, can create a culture of hospitality that will benefit the church in many ways. What about your church members? Are they noticing those near them in worship? Are they paying attention to those by themselves at the coffee hour?

Other areas to consider closely are the processes used in the church. For example, think about donations received by the church. When donations are received, are they acknowledged at different points during the year? Is there a letter of thanks sent out with the financial statement that includes an update on exciting ways the funds are being used? At the end of the year, is a final statement prepared for tax purposes? Does it conform to the requirements of the Internal Revenue Service? If your church has developed the option of making a donation online, how easy is it? Take time to make a donation online yourself sometime, and then consider whether it was simple or difficult. The experience you are having is the reason people will give or become impatient and choose not to complete the transaction. The details may seem unimportant, but sometimes you can quantify the impact they have on the congregation. When those who donate to your congregation know that they can trust your processes, whether financial or in some other arena, they will be far more likely to make future investments of time and money that you will be blessed to receive.

There are all sorts of "corners" to consider and so many opportunities to feel the impact of small improvements. It may be the way we make announcements, what the restrooms look like, or the margins of the bulletin. Think of the host of things that shape, in a subtle way, a person's impression of you or your church. Most of us do fairly well with 90 percent of our work, but it may be the remaining 10 percent "around the corners" that will make the difference.

MEASURE TO LEARN, NOT JUDGE

The current focus on setting numerical goals for ministry and reporting on the results is not new, though it is now greatly expanded. In the past, virtually all the goals churches set had to do with money. The most obvious example is the annual budget. A budget is a goal that the church works all year to achieve, monitors closely, and reports on regularly. Usually no one in the congregation gives more attention to monitoring and achieving those goals than the pastor. We now give the same attention to some *people categories*, but the concept is essentially the same.

This expansion of goals, monitoring, and reporting, however, could easily miss the point as we have often done with finances. Any time the conversations turn to setting goals, many people think of such efforts as a way to set a standard on which they must eventually report and by which they will be judged. That may happen, but it should not be the primary use for such metrics. The most important benefit of defining numerical goals is that the goals become the opportunity to shape planning that your church already needs. Such goal setting works even better if you do not try to do everything at the same time but rather select those areas around which there is both need and passion.

Progress comes when we have a goal toward which we are moving. Former Pixar storyboard artist Emma Coats recently shared via Twitter twenty-two rules of storytelling she learned while working for Pixar. One of the rules is to "come up with your ending before you figure out your middle."[1] It does not help to begin talking about what we should do until we have a clear definition of what we want our activities to accomplish. Our focus on setting targets and planning to reach them does not suggest that our goals will capture all we hope to accomplish. The Spirit works in amazing ways to accomplish more than any statistics can ever reflect, but usually the Spirit accomplishes those unexpected signs and wonders when we are generating our own holy energy through prayer and hard work.

Reporting matters but is never the true purpose of your efforts. The numbers you report may show you reached or exceeded your goals. They are just as likely to show that you missed your goals. Remember that most churches do not achieve 100 percent of their budget goals each year, but that does not keep them from setting new budget goals for the next year, working hard to achieve the goals, monitoring the results diligently, and reporting the results.

The real benefit of the results you report comes from what you *learned* from the results. Perhaps you set a goal to reach sixty children in Sunday school, and you fell short. But if you learned that the teachers need more training, that worship and Sunday school need to be coordinated better, that you need teams of teachers, or that your age groupings are too broad, your "failure" may be the beginning of fruitfulness that will benefit children for years to come.

But, you might ask, isn't it discouraging to set goals you do not reach? It is discouraging only if you permit conversations to focus solely on success and failure. No matter what the numbers indicate, you should always ask the following three questions:

- What did you learn?

- What actions have you taken on the basis of what you learned?

- What results have occurred from those actions?

If you can identify what you have learned (which shows you are paying attention), name the changes made from those learnings (which shows you intend to improve), and illustrate that you have made progress despite falling short of the original goal (which shows you are acting on the right learnings), your efforts will bear fruit no matter what the current numbers indicate. Whenever there are conversations to review numbers, always insist that prior to the conversation everyone have both the numbers and a narrative of the learnings thus far, changes made or planned where necessary, and progress from any of those changes.

Fruitfulness is vastly different from success. Goals help fruitfulness, but fruitfulness does not require attainment of all our goals. Fruitfulness is not about personal or congregational glory but the advancement of God's reign. Church leaders care about results because results are ways to go beyond merely doing good ministry to active participation in God's hope for all to experience the abundant life revealed in Jesus Christ.

COUNT PEOPLE AS CAREFULLY AS MONEY

At a recent gathering, clergy and laity from several congregations were asked how they keep track of their attendance each Sunday and how they keep up with who is attending. A vigorous debate ensued. Some reported how they monitor the numbers and keep track of people attending, but the energy was with those who did not attempt either task. The churches represented tended to be smaller and mid-size churches.

Common responses included:

There are only a few of us, so why count? Do you know how much trouble it would be to keep up with who is attending? We don't have any staff to do that. We are more like family, so to count doesn't seem right. We count the attendance, but there is no way we could keep up with which people are present.

At first what they said seemed to make sense to others. Perhaps there are churches where counting is not a part of the culture and other places where there are no staff or volunteers to make sure such monitoring takes place.

But then someone raised another question: "What do you

do about the money collected in the offering?" No one seemed to understand the question. So it was asked again: "If counting is not a part of how you do things, and if you do not have adequate staff or volunteers to count, what in the world do you do with the money contributed each week?"

The answer then came quickly: "Well, we count it." And the questioner continued, asking how they remembered who gave the money. "We record it." How do you get it to the bank? "We prepare a deposit and take it to the bank." And when the questioner inquired whether they do this just once a month since it is so hard to get things counted and tracked, they replied, "No. We do it every week."

Interesting. Such practices may tell us about priorities and why most churches are reaching fewer people through worship year after year.

It is curious that some feel their small size makes it hard to monitor attendance. When I was a pastor of small membership churches, I found those to be the easiest places to keep track both of numbers and people. One person can get the "head-count" simply by "counting heads." And after the service, the pastor or any one of many laity can put check marks by those present on a list of members. I remember running into a church member on a street corner one day. He said, "Pastor, good to see you. I know I have not been to church for two or three weeks." I replied, "Actually, it's five, but who's counting!" We had a good laugh.

In reality, there are things we may resist when it comes to paying careful attention to those responding to God's love through worship, but we readily adopt such practices when it comes to the care we offer to those who give money to the church. The donors and their gifts need careful attention, but so do the people who through each occasion of worship are "lifting their hands" to say they want to grow in their discipleship.

Such confusion of priorities takes place in larger churches as well. One congregation received new members on only one Sunday per month. As more people were joining, some could not be present on the designated Sunday. The pastor wanted to involve church staff in considering the idea that opportunities for people to join be extended to additional Sundays—for staff had several roles related to receiving new members. The pastor expected some staff concerns about logistics but was not prepared for the all-out resistance to the proposed change.

Instead of pushing back, the pastor surprised the staff by saying, "You are right. It is just too much trouble to receive new members more often." And then he got the staff's attention quickly. "In fact, I am so convinced by your argument that I think we should extend the wisdom of the once-a-month idea. We can save tremendous time and effort if we only receive offerings on one designated Sunday per month."

As long as you count the money, keep track of who is giving it, and report regularly how you are doing financially, then at least do the same for the people God leads to your house of worship.

And do not stop with the recording of names and numbers. What do these records tell you? After a member of my small church had missed several Sundays, we inquired to be sure there was not illness in their family or other serious problems. When what had traditionally been a "low attendance Sunday" suddenly had the largest attendance of the summer, the pastors discovered the power of involving young people in the leadership of worship.

Numbers and records represent the people God has given to us—and God calls us to be faithful with this treasure, whether it is large or small.

CHAPTER 4

COMMUNICATE, COMMUNICATE, COMMUNICATE

SEE YOURSELF AS THE CHIEF COMMUNICATION OFFICER

If one had to name a single, all-purpose instrument of leadership, it would be communication.

—John W. Gardner

Effective leaders are good communicators. They understand the importance of communication in all its forms and spend much time at the task. This communication is always two-way, receiving as well as giving information and feelings. Doris Kearns Goodwin found in her studies of presidential leadership that leaders can "possess all the other attributes and still fail to have an impact" without skill in communication.[1]

"The essence of leadership—what we do with 98 percent of our time—is communication," says Peter Senge. "To master any management practice, we must start by bringing discipline to the domain in which we spend most of our time, the domain of words."[2]

Indeed, there is no way for leaders to avoid communication. Even the absence of direct and planned communication sends a powerful message, almost always negative. If words are not being communicated, actions are. The question for leaders is not if they will communicate, but what and how to communicate.

However, even leaders who know that communication is important do not always see themselves as the chief communications officer. Deciding to frame your leadership around the communicator role requires an intentional choice to view virtually every aspect of leadership from the vantage point of the chief "storyteller" of the congregation.

Just as our sermons must have a narrative, so must our leadership. A sermon moves in a way that people can follow. Leadership is always about a story. It is the story of God's saving work from the beginning of time. It is the story of God's decisive action in Christ and the witness of the entire Christian church over the centuries. It is often the story of a denominational tradition out of which your congregation emerged. And, particularly, it is the story of your congregation's community of faith from its inception (not simply since your arrival) and a never-wavering passion to do God's will and especially discern the next faithful step God has for your congregation.

It is a story of success and failure, radical obedience and shameful disobedience. The mountains and valleys remind the people of the joys and sorrows that go with seeking to know and do God's will. It reminds people of the high price we pay for periods of apathy and how self-defeating it is to live off the past or try to recreate the past. It preserves and cherishes the past but points to the future as the proper realm for the current congregation.

Leadership is far more than doing your job well. A pastor can perform all the many tasks of ministry in ways that win praise and provide personal satisfaction while, at the same time, not helping the congregation take their next faithful step. Even an extremely dedicated and professional pastor who ministers for years may not necessarily further the congregation on its pilgrimage.

Fruitful leaders use communication to draw from the past, describe the present, and envision the future in ways that unify God's people and motivate and inspire them. People need a picture of where they have been, where they are now, and where God is calling them to go. The story becomes the congregation's story in ways that permit them to tell it as well. Most important is for all to see themselves and their discipleship as part of the story.

The story will often be uplifting, but sometimes it is sobering. A leader whose credibility is strong, whose love for the people is unquestioned, and whose default position is always to presume grace instead of judgment will be able to name hard realities as easily as celebrating successes. The leader is not the main character in the story, but the leader has special responsibility to make sure the story is communicated often and in varying ways and that it is appropriate for the circumstances. The leader also pays special attention to how well the story is unfolding.

Here is where the two-way nature of communication becomes so important. Leaders tell the story not because they are wiser than anyone else. The leader is the storyteller partly by position but just as much so because the leader often is the one who has access to more information and people and spends more time thinking and praying about God's vision than others. But that does not mean that the leader's interpretation of the story is always correct. The best storytellers pay attention to how the story resonates with others since no story is told unless it is heard. The listening is not for agreement so much as whether the story fits with the church's history, current realities, and future opportunities.

Seeing oneself as the chief communication officer transforms tasks that may previously have been performed with little enthusiasm. Someone reminds you that your weekly newsletter message is due. Now, what might have seemed a burden before becomes a wonderful opportunity. You are excited that you have yet another opportunity to tell the story, or, more likely, to highlight some specific part of the story. Or you are invited to stop by on Saturday morning to bring greetings and offer a prayer for a regional denomination group having their meeting at your church. Perhaps in the past that would have seemed an intrusion on your Saturday morning. Now, it becomes another chance to remind the visitors (and, more importantly, your own members present) of some aspect of the church's story and vision. Now announcements and sermons can connect to the larger story. Conversations during the week provide opportunities to ask questions and share news about the story. Committee agendas come alive when the various items are seen in light of where God is calling the church to go. Every task invites the chief communication officer to lift the vision and tell the story.

PREACH WELL

When drivers in the United States are asked to rate their ability to operate a vehicle, it turns out we all think we are above average, usually a seven or higher on a ten-point scale. People will say this regardless of age. They rate themselves highly even with driving records that indicate they are anything but above-average drivers. Psychologists call this phenomenon "illusory superiority." While we can be very good at rating others correctly, we almost always think of ourselves as above the standard.[3]

While the authors of this book have never done a study to verify our suspicions, we suspect that preachers may suffer from illusory superiority. Talk to pastors about their preaching, and you will rarely hear them say, "One of the problems with our church is that I am such an average preacher. In fact, I am below average." Talk to the people who attend their churches, and you will often hear them make a quick diagnosis of why the church is languishing. "One of the big problems is the preaching. The pastor is a wonderful person but not an engaging speaker."

Why would the topic of preaching be included in a book on leadership? Preaching is a primary leadership arena in the church. It is where people come to know the person who is their pastor. Listening to the sermon, they determine whether their pastor has a strong intellect and whether she or he understands the issues that impact the world and the personal lives of those in the congregation and surrounding community. Through preaching, people hear the pastor's guiding theology and his or her ability to apply the teaching of scripture to daily life. It is while listening to sermons that people often decide whether or not they can trust their pastor with sensitive issues in their lives and whether or not the pastor is someone who would be a dependable steward of the financial resources they may choose to give the church.

Nowhere do leaders have a more consistent communication vehicle than the sermon. At least once a week, pastors get to speak to their congregations. Pastors can impart their vision for the church and the significance of the church's goals for the local community. Leaders of other organizations would be envious of such an opportunity to stay connected to their constituents and speak in ways that guide the course of their organizations every seven days.

This is why pastors have to be good preachers if they are going to be good leaders. It is essential that pastors learn the skills of verbal communication that will enhance their message. They must also remember that unlike public speakers, they have material that has stood the test of time. Church members are not looking for pastors who entertain or dazzle them with their speaking ability. They are hoping that the pastor can clearly articulate the word of God in a way that will encourage and remind them of the reasons they give their time, talent, and money to the church.

The congregation is best served when the preacher sees the task of preaching as an opportunity to lead people on a personal and corporate journey of faith. They want to know how God is present in their world. Because preachers are not the only people suffering from illusory superiority, members of the church need to hear words of truth that sometimes convict people regarding the state of their soul or the state of their community. When a sermon comforts those who are dealing with loss or helps them see God's presence in a period of suffering, they understand why their faith and their church are so central to their lives. Strongly rooted in the word of God, dependable preaching provides Christians with an essential fortitude that they seek in weekly worship. When preaching is compromised by a lack of preparation or by the speaker's distracting habits or through the sheer tedium created by those who do not expend extra effort on a sermon due to overconfidence in their skill, the pastor is compromised in ways they may not understand. Good preaching enables church members to feel assured that their pastor will lead the church in ways that are competent, faithful, and fruitful.

BECOME AN EXCELLENT SPEAKER

If you are going to be the chief communication officer—the storyteller for the congregation—then it is essential to continue to grow as an excellent speaker.

Aristotle named three elements necessary for a successful argument: ethos, pathos, and logos. *Ethos* refers to the personhood and integrity of the speaker. *Pathos* refers to the connection with those to whom one is speaking. And *logos* is about the rational argument and logic of the substance of your presentation.

Ethos

Just as credibility is essential for all leadership, it is critical to effective communication. How people view the speaker makes a huge difference in whether they will be moved by the speaker. Some call this the "ethical proof" factor. Leaders with high ethical proof are seen by listeners as someone who understands them, shares their values, and has integrity. Leaders with low ethical proof are persons listeners know little about or, in the case of those with lowest ethical proof, are seen as people who do not care for them or share their values. So what people know about the speaker ahead of time, and particularly their experience with the speaker, will tend to determine how effective the speaker is in communicating with an audience.

Pathos

Pathos reminds us that the audience determines if communication takes place. Therefore, excellent speakers begin not with their content but with the makeup of the recipients of their message. In some ways, this is what happens when a pastor walks through the sanctuary on Saturday and pictures who is likely to be sitting in various spots the next day at worship. Those names and their stories help the preacher speak more compellingly to the needs of the actual people who are present. This is an example of the importance of "outside to inside" thinking rather than "inside to outside" thinking. In the latter, the speaker focuses almost exclusively on "what I want to say." A better approach is to begin with picturing those who will hear the message and then frame the same content in ways that make it more likely they will hear it. Such a sermon is less likely to begin with "I would submit" and more likely to begin with "Have you ever had a time when...?"

Logos

The message still needs to make sense. The information shared needs to be true, and the implications drawn from that information should be logical. Arguments need to be sound and illustrations appropriate to the points being made. Logos is where most pastoral leaders put the majority of their effort. In some ways, that is what we are educated to do. We want to be right, and being right is certainly better than being wrong. But being right is not enough. We need to find ways for the truth we speak to be right for those who hear our message. Our speaking must be rational and thoughtful, but Aristotle reminds us that we need something more to be excellent speakers.

One reason our logical arguments do not convince as well as we hope is what some call a "confirmation bias." This refers to how people tend to receive new information through some mental filters. People tend to pick up very well on those things they hear and read that confirm what they already believe. They are much more likely to remember such new information. It makes them stronger in their original belief. On the other hand, new information that challenges what they already believe does not have the same impact. It tends not to be remembered and usually does not change their opinion. A wise leader of an earlier generation once said, "What logic did not put into someone's head, logic will not take out!"

An exercise may help you. Make a list of all the many ways in which you communicate through planned speaking or writing in the course of a week. Then, beside that list put three columns for ethos, pathos, and logos. Which of these three aspects of speaking get most of your attention as you prepare for each of your communication opportunities? Whatever the results, you now have a good worksheet for enhancing your speaking by giving more attention to those aspects often neglected.

MAKE HEROES OF OTHERS

One of the pioneers of veterinary medicine was Dr. Mark L. Morris. He was a founder and the first president of the American Animal Hospital Association in 1933, and he constructed one of the first small animal hospitals in the United States in 1929. He became internationally known as the father of small-animal clinical nutrition with his development of dietary dog and cat foods known as Prescription Diet. He also founded the Morris Animal Foundation in 1948 to sponsor health studies for dogs, cats, horses, and other animals. Actress Betty White has served as president and spokesperson for the foundation for many years.

Dr. Morris lived to the age of ninety-two. At his memorial service, which Lovett attended, a knowledgeable veterinarian said that 99 percent of the veterinarians in the world knew of Dr. Morris. He went on to say that veterinarians loved Dr. Morris because he made heroes out of them. Beginning with Dr. Morris's first innovations in formulating dietary foods for sick dogs and cats, the veterinarians were able to take those diets, use them beneficially for the animals they were treating, and thereby become beloved by their clients.

Good leaders make heroes out of many people and find their satisfaction in the fulfillment of the vision, not in personal recognition. Therefore, these leaders are freed to recognize others and to seek actively to make sure that others become the heroes.

There are many ways to recognize heroes. Here are four that are easily accomplished:

> *Share ideas generously.* If you have good ideas that will help others, share them. Churches often lack policies and procedures that other nonprofits have readily available. If you have a personnel manual, position descriptions, best practices for the way finances are managed, or

administrative policies that others could easily adopt, it will be a great help if you will share them. You may have a sermon series that received a great response in your church. Share everything with other churches, including the sermons, visual aids, musical selections, website information, and other materials. If you had a great children's program over the summer, you can share not only the curriculum, but also any decorations, sets, or other aids that were used in your setting. The list of possibilities is large. Don't wait for people to come to you and ask. Seek out others who might be hesitant to ask but might readily accept if you initiate the offer. When you share these items, tell them there is no need to credit you or your church. Your joy will be found in their success.

Share your time. Often the best learning occurs on a peer-to-peer basis. When others call to ask you a question, schedule a phone call or invite them to stop by at a time conducive to a conversation. Typically people who call are hoping that they will receive more than a quick answer to an easy problem. There is usually something going on that is important. It could be a problem that they do not know how to solve or an opportunity they fear will get past them. Sometimes it is a personal matter that they do not know where to take for conversation. Your willingness to mentor them, even for an hour, can often set up another leader for success who would not have found it without outside counsel. One key to giving your time is to schedule it when it works on your calendar. Most people who have a real issue they want to discuss are more than happy to work around your schedule if they can simply have access to your listening ear, your thoughts, and your ideas. Once the meeting is over, put a note on your calendar to call or e-mail after a week or two to follow up. It is amazing how encouraging it is to receive the interest of others we respect.

Celebrate. If you are holding a staff meeting or leadership council meeting, always take time to celebrate what others are doing that serves the mission of the congregation. Allow the group to recognize the events and people, and allow time to tell stories that spotlight the accomplishments of those who are making a difference. If you find that some people receive regular feedback and other people or ministry areas are rarely celebrated, take time to look closely at their work and fruitfulness so you will be prepared to speak a personal word the next time the group gathers. There are many reasons why we do not celebrate some people who work diligently and produce real results. Some are more introverted and fly under the radar of those around them. Others play unseen supportive roles that make the people up front look great. Make sure to celebrate these people.

If they are not present at the meetings you attend, take time to send them a handwritten note thanking them for their efforts. Demonstrate in what you write that you understand how their contribution connects to the greater mission of the congregation. Sometimes it is nice to sound a bit conspiratorial: "Sue, you work so diligently and quietly that many may not be aware of all the good work you do around here. But you and I both know that your work blesses people in our church. Last week I noticed.... I just wanted to write this in case you forgot how important you are to all of us..." Often, people treasure these notes for years after they receive them. Celebrations remind people that they are heroes.

Notice. Tom once sat next to a high school principal at graduation in a rural town. The students were slowly coming down from the school building to the football field for commencement. Tom said to the principal, "I am so impressed at how nice you have made this graduation. The decorations are all brand new. The stage looks professionally arranged. The balloons and streamers communicate that this really is an important event."

The principal smiled, "Thank you for noticing. We do spend a lot of time planning graduation, and we want it to look really nice. In this county, only 44 percent of our students will go on to college. Most will work in jobs where they will one day retire without a luncheon or a gold watch. Several years ago it dawned on me that there would be only two potential celebrations for many of these young people in their lifetime. One is this graduation. The other is a wedding, if they choose to get married. So we spend a little extra money on this event, and I am glad that was evident to you." This principal noticed something essential about her students. Thanks to her efforts, at graduation the whole community properly celebrated their accomplishment. They became heroes for the day.

Think of what it might mean for your ministry if you could turn ordinary people into heroes and celebrate what they do and who they are. How might this change the way you relate to others? What could you learn from the work of Dr. Morris or the high school principal about what you could do with leaders in your church that would help make them heroes in the eyes of those with whom they work? What could you do for teachers that would make them heroes with their students? How could you help improve the ministry of staff members that would enhance how they are regarded by members of the congregation? Pay attention each day to how you can make someone a hero.

SPEAK THE WHOLE TRUTH (TOM)

Jesus lived in a time of bad news: Roman occupation, splits in the Temple between Pharisees and Sadducees, Essenes and Zealots, religious people who refused to get along as much as they refused to get together. It was a time of poverty, disease, and rebellion. In the midst of that, Jesus came to his home synagogue and read the scroll of Isaiah:

> "The Spirit of the Lord is upon me,
>> because he has anointed me
>>> to bring good news to the poor.
> He has sent me to proclaim release to the captives
>> and recovery of sight to the blind,
>>> to let the oppressed go free,
> to proclaim the year of the Lord's favor." (Luke 4:18-19)

He was telling them that after all those years and disappointments with Assyrians, Babylonians, Greeks, and Romans, after all those bad kings, after all the high altars and other ways people had forsaken God, after all the false prophets and tragic endings for true prophets, God was, unbelievably, still in the good news business.

Leaders remind people of good news even in the worst of times. Primarily the good news is that despite ourselves, God is still in our midst, still up to something, still pushing and prodding us so that we can find a life that has love and joy to the fullest. God is still ahead of us, pointing to where the good stuff is to be found.

A few years ago I was in Sierra Leone, Africa, with members of the church I serve. There was a lot of bad news in that country. Maternal death rates were high. Malaria cases were astounding. The mortality rate for infants and children under five was alarming. A woman who leads the work of the church was sharing the good news about the impact of a campaign called Imagine No

59

Malaria. As a result of the church's efforts, malaria had declined in the villages and towns that used the mosquito nets offered through this program. Here was this competent young adult with her facts and figures, whose team had discovered how to get pastors and imams to participate in bed net distributions and remind their people that the body is a temple and should be protected. She shared statistics about lives saved and how the World Health Organization had finally awakened to the impact of the church's medical system, including the hospital with which we were partners. As she shared her good news, my heart felt so full of love for the church and its generous, compassionate nature that I could barely stand it. I am as inspired now as I write this as I was then, and that is the point. There is something about good news that kindles the inner fire. Leaders must share good news because, God knows, we need it.

By now you may be thinking that I am one of those people who want to turn every leader into a walking thank-you note and every talk into a happy report.

Leaders also have to tell the whole truth, which will also include bad news. Leaders share the truth even when it hurts, even when it does not make us proud, even when it sounds like terrible news. You must tell people the truth about the world and the church and its leaders and followers because the Christ who came to preach good news to the poor and recovery of sight to the blind, the One who came to set the prisoners free, also said that we should know the truth and the truth would set us free. So speak in loving and gracious ways, but give people the unflinching facts about our life together, the suffering of the world, and how many still do not know Christ as the numbers of those who have no religion grow and those who call themselves Christ followers diminish. And don't shade, hide, or stretch the truth, because the truth is powerful just as it is. While good news can inspire, bad news often has the power to convict, which most people need to experience often.

60

Leaders must do this kind of thing in the church because the hard truth can be the precursor to repentance, and repentance is a time when God can truly get ahold of us. When the Spirit of the living God falls afresh on us, then transformation can begin. That is when bad news becomes good news. This is why the truth is a form of good news even when the particular truth you are telling sounds like bad news. Be aware that people do not like bad news. They may shoot the messenger, but if you fear that, you should have thought about it before you became a leader in the church.

Recently I received a voicemail from a young man whose mother is an alcoholic. They had never used that word before, preferring to call it her "drinking issue." He had finally gotten to the point where he realized something must be done. He did what leaders do. He pulled his family together for an honest conversation. He sought guidance from a counselor. He rallied the family to hold an intervention with his mom. He called to tell me that his mom agreed to enter a rehabilitation center. He asked me to pray for her. Because they are dealing with the whole truth for the first time, it is now possible that bad news, finally confronted, will lead to good news, finally experienced.

People need leaders to encourage them with the good news of what Christ is doing in the world. And they need you to tell them the whole truth that includes the bad news of why we need Jesus in the first place. God's leaders tell the whole truth—the good news in all its forms—sometimes affirming and sometimes challenging. The consistent message we maintain is the amazing news that God is still at work, despite us and with us, and that is the best news of all.

CHAPTER 5

REDEEM CONFLICT

ENGAGE CONFLICT (TOM)

A few years after becoming a pastor, I had an uncomfortable conversation with a long-tenured church member. It was clear we were never going to find a middle ground on the topic at hand. Our discussion was eroding into an argument.

In those days I was convinced that if people would just take time to talk things over, they could always come to some form of agreement. Conflict was to be avoided; but if it presented itself, I would be utterly placid. But as we continued talking, I found that I was having a number of responses that were hard to control. My heart was starting to beat faster. I was getting more agitated as the other person pointed out perceived significant flaws in the plan I supported. I became defensive. My words became terse. I even raised my voice. I was amazed that anyone could be so stubborn and insistent on having their own way.

At the end of the conversation, we had a deeper disagreement than when we began. More important, rather than diffusing the situation, my defensive posture served only to confirm the church member's worst assumptions about my leadership and the plan that was of such great concern. While I may have been right about the topic of discussion, I was dismissive of important concerns and possible alternatives that may also have had merit. We parted on very poor terms.

I wanted to reach out to this person, but my discomfort was hard to overcome. The thought of additional conflict made me queasy. I started to call but found reasons to procrastinate. When I finally made contact, I learned that the damage was done. I never succeeded in involving this person in the church again.

At first I felt unsettled at the lack of resolution. Then I felt guilty over losing a church member. I agonized over this for many weeks.

One night I had a dream. I was at a college and was standing outside a large house used for a campus ministry group. When I entered, there was a Franciscan friar in a brown habit and sandals. He was a kind and joyful man who was lighting the first of many candles that were placed all over the room. I could tell that he was in a hurry, with other tasks to complete. There were dozens more to light. I offered to help him, and he gratefully handed me a candle. I lit candle after candle as the dark room turned to light. Finally I went to the mantel over the fireplace. I tried to light the final candle. I knew the time was short. People were starting to arrive, and I could hear their voices approaching. No matter what I tried, I could not get the final candle to light. My heart rate increased along with my anxiety. I was practically breaking out in a sweat as I pried the wax away from the wick and held the flame to it. Nothing worked. The candle remained unlit. When my frustration was at its height, I felt the friar place his hand on my shoulder and ask, "What is the matter?"

Exasperated, I answered, "Father, I'm sorry. No matter what I try, I cannot get this candle to light." Smiling, he said, "Then leave it alone. It is not yours to light. Someone else will take care of it. But look around you. Look at all the candles that are lit." As I looked about, I saw the room illuminated by dozens of candles. The light reflected off the faces of those entering, who were smiling and happy to see each other. The scene was beautiful.

Then I woke up.

Both the conflict with the member and the dream have stuck with me for many years. I learned how uncomfortable I was with disagreement and how prone people can be to fight or flight instincts that highjack higher-level thinking and speaking. Convicted by discomfort, I knew I had to mature if I was ever going to grow as a leader. Conflict is a normative part of leadership and the human experience. Bad outcomes happen when we embrace it too quickly, and when we avoid it completely. The ability to be humble, to listen carefully, and to honor others with patience, even when I strongly disagree with them, were qualities I learned I would have to embrace in order to lead well and fruitfully.

I also learned that sometimes you have to commit people to God's hands. You are not a failure if you lose someone whose personal vision differs from the vision your congregation has discerned to be God's next faithful step. God has others who can be their pastors and other journeys they can choose to take—which may well be as good as the ones you are offering. The key is to manage the conflict in such a way that you minimize the regrets that come when community is sometimes broken and to keep your eyes focused on the good that still surrounds you.

GET COMFORTABLE WITH UNCOMFORTABLE CONVERSATIONS

People like their church to be nice. They want nice music, nice sermons, and nice conversations between nice people. Other parts of their lives have conflict. The boss at work can be difficult. Their next-door neighbor may be angry and demanding. Their child's school bus driver may be grouchy. Their cat may scratch them. But church is supposed to be nice. The picture of Jesus on the wall makes him look very nice. There he is, gently holding a lost lamb. Another shows him greeting smiling children. Even the Bible says: "A gentle answer turns away wrath, but a harsh word stirs up anger" (Proverbs 15:1 NIV).

And let's face it, nice is . . . , well . . . , nice.

The problem is that many churches are dying of terminal niceness. Some are dying because the church has an inward focus and does not see the spiritual, social, or economic needs of the surrounding community. But it might make members of the congregation uncomfortable if someone pointed out that they were too comfortable, so nothing is said. Other churches are dying because they ignore or do not address members' destructive behaviors, which break the unity of the body of Christ and leave people with a negative experience of the church that will take years to overcome. Even so, it seems out of concert with Jesus's admonition to turn the other cheek to make someone uncomfortable by mentioning these challenges.

Unfortunately, even as the people in the church place a high value on being nice, at any given time there are situations that leaders simply must address:

- A husband going through a separation spreads gossip about his wife through social media while insisting on being the head usher each week at worship.

- The traditional music director and the church band's lead vocalist snipe about each other in private while extolling how much more worshipful music at their service is compared to the other services.

- A long-term church member complains about the weeklong hypothermia shelter for individuals who are homeless, stating that *those bums have no business in this building.*

- A mother's depression becomes so severe that there is concern for the care of her daughter.

On many days, the job of being a leader is just not very nice. Leaders have to become comfortable with uncomfortable conversations. Throughout the Bible, leaders had to say hard things to others. Moses had to point out those idols people made while he was up on the mountain talking to the Lord. Nathan had to tell David that he crossed the line. Deborah had to tell the general that he was being a coward. John the Baptist called the crowd a *brood of vipers*. The list of people in the Bible saying hard things goes on and on. That was before preachers started sermons with funny stories.

And Jesus, well, he simply had a gift of saying things that brought discomfort. He called religious officials *whitewashed tombs*. He told his favorite disciple, "Get behind me, Satan." He said that his true family was not the group of biological relatives questioning his sanity but those who followed his teaching. That is but a small sample of uncomfortable things Jesus said to others.

Let's be clear. Jesus never told us to be nice to one another. He did tell us to love one another. And love sometimes requires us to say hard things that may make us uncomfortable so that unhealthy situations can begin to change. Leaders understand that this goes along with their role.

Sometimes we have to tell church members that they need a season of rest from their volunteer responsibilities while they rededicate energy to personal life and issues. We have to tell staff members that they cannot undermine colleagues while being paid by the church. Spiritual leaders have to challenge gently and even call out those who speak from an unkind or unsympathetic heart so antithetical to the spirit of Christ. Sometimes leaders have to point out neglect and offer assistance and aid but ultimately involve others if neglect continues.

Leaders realize that the warning about these moments is in the fine print of the calling they felt when they took up the privilege and responsibility of their positions. Great leaders learn to say hard things in a calm and humble manner that communicates their concern for the listener as well as others affected by the issue being raised. They learn to control the anxiety that accompanies conflict so that their emotions will not negatively impact their thoughts and speech. They also carry the desire of Christ to see people experience love, repentance, and restoration rather than discipline and exclusion from the community.

Just as wood cannot be finished without sandpaper, all organizations, especially churches, cannot reach their potential without uncomfortable conversations.

KEEP AT IT

Most problems do not get resolved in one meeting, no matter what the minutes say. This is especially true when changing a congregational system. If the church board is moving to a different governing style, if the staff is restructured or the board size reduced, there will be a need to find ways to return to the issue after making the formal decision. Once a decision is made, people have to get used to its ramifications. Churches have to discard old habits in order to begin new practices appropriate to the new system. Leaders may have to calm some anger and fear. It is essential for members to acknowledge their apprehensions, ask questions, and appropriately express concerns, while the leaders continue to remind everyone of the reasons decisions were made.

Leaders live in a tension. If we capitulate whenever people want to go back to the old way of doing things, there will be no ongoing transformation. Old problems will linger unaddressed. If we do not allow people to express their discomfort and resolve their concerns, we will create mistrust and grudges that will impact the relationships that give churches meaning.

It is important to respond quickly to the concerns people have, especially about change. Discontent spreads like a virus on a cruise ship. Do not confuse the extent of the concern in the congregation with the depth of frustration in the individual do-ing the sharing. This is particularly true when people claim that many unnamed "others" are concerned, and you need to do some-thing immediately. In this moment, stay focused on the issues rather than the personalities involved. Ask the person to state the specific nature of the concern. Request the person share exactly what was said rather than their interpretation of what was said. The goal is not to split hairs but to get to the root of the concern. Historians know that the most reliable history is found in source documents. These are the original works upon which religions are built or to which systems of governance are anchored. Over time, source documents are interpreted in a variety of ways, depending on the outlook and agendas of later commentators. The leader's task is to find the original concern and honor it by bringing it to resolution. Bypassing the commentary about the concern can bring clarity and save hours of unnecessary conversation.

This is another opportunity to assume the best about every-one involved. This sometimes can be accomplished by register-ing gentle surprise along with a compliment. "I'm surprised to hear that. I remember when John [a widely trusted member] voted for this change and said it would be difficult but would help us. I have always trusted John and his opinions. His sup-port made me more comfortable with the change."

Remember that everything you say will be quoted to others who will quote it to others. By sharing complimentary state-ments that are true, you will keep everyone focused on the issue before you rather than the hurt feelings caused when negative intentions are ascribed to others. Also ask if people are aware of the process used to make the decision. Carefully sharing the identified problem, alternatives considered, rationale for the fi-nal decision, and who approved it often helps people see the change in a fresh way. Being transparent demonstrates that there is no conspiracy afoot. Some printed materials used in the delib-erations may be helpful to share.

It is important to demonstrate that whenever a serious concern is brought to your attention, you will deal with it directly. Some people want to triangulate their discontent. When this happens, open the door widely. Tell the person bringing concerns to you from others that the concerns raised are important and that you want to talk directly with those who are frustrated. It is amazing how quickly "so many people" often becomes a list of one to three names. Again, it is essential for the leader to remain a non-anxious presence in the midst of what can be a highly frustrating topic. Leaders spend weeks of time preparing for big changes. They work for consensus before the vote is taken. It is easy to become offended when it feels as if someone moved the finish line and added an additional mile to the race through complaint time. Keep in mind that the greater the magnitude of change, the further out the finish line is moved. Do not become agitated. This is part of the change process.

Set up a meeting with those troubled by the change. Try to do this individually or in small groups rather than inviting everyone to come at once. Crowds are rarely conducive to constructive conversation.

Share that you respect their opinions and want to hear from them personally. Some will say hard things. But you gain the opportunity to clarify the change and its rationale. When people know that you will contact them in a kind and professional manner and hear them out, they begin to change patterns of communication.

Finally, it is important to move people from problem identification to solution generation. When possible, ask those unhappy with some plans to share ways they might solve the original problem. If they are upset with a new ministry to help poor children, ask them what God has put on their hearts as the best way to serve these children. Assume they care as much about the children as you do. If they are against starting a new worship service to reach younger people, ask them to pray about another approach that would permit the church to achieve the same goal of reaching younger people. Keep the focus on the original goal of the decision they question rather than merely defending the decision.

Over time you may discover that your presumption of the best from complainers is misplaced for a few members. That is sad but a reality. While you need to stay connected to everyone with pastoral concern and respect, you probably need to invest more time with those who demonstrate genuine openness to the church's mission beyond their personal preferences. And, yet, your genuine attention to all who bring concerns and questions will go a long way toward a strong support for the mission and, perhaps, new aspects to strengthening that mission.

BE HUMBLE AND ASSERTIVE

"So let no one boast about human leaders," says Paul (1 Corinthians 3:21a). The experience out of which this verse comes is a good illustration of why humility can be such a challenge for leaders, particularly gifted leaders. Not only do leaders face the human tendency toward self-importance, but they also encounter followers who often mistake the leader for the larger purpose served by the leader.

Paul addresses the Corinthians who were boasting in human leaders. In the midst of sharp divisions and conflicts, they had chosen sides by lifting up different leaders. One boasted in Paul; another, in Apollos; yet another, in Cephas.

This boasting mistakes the role of the Christian leader. Such promotion of a human leader misplaces the loyalty of Christians and misinterprets how leaders relate to followers. Paul reminds the Corinthians that they do not belong to a particular leader (or party, ideology, or politics). They belong to Christ. When leaders forget this lesson, they get into trouble. When leaders operate without a theological grounding for their leadership, there is weakness and the form of conflict Corinthians experienced.

Christian Humility

Christian humility is grounded, writes Joan Chittister, in our knowing that every gift we have is God's gift, not our own possession.[1] Thus, we are stewards of each gift; each has been given so that it may be used in the service of others. She reminds us also that the gifts of our sisters and brothers are God's gifts as well.

Therefore, leaders lead, knowing that others are not beneath or above them. Leaders know themselves as those with much to receive and much to give. Humility is fundamentally a recognition of what it is we have to give and to receive. It is not, as we have prayed so often, a correction to thinking of ourselves "more highly than we ought to think." Neither is it thinking of ourselves "less highly than we ought to think."

Our gifts are God's. To reject God's gifts in us is not humility. Failing to affirm and use those good gifts in our leadership may be the most unfaithful way of twisting the virtue of humility.

The wonderful truth about humility is that we come to know ourselves truly, acknowledging both our limitations and gifts. Just as we have much to learn, we also have much to offer. While we are rightly reluctant to assert a supposed superior wisdom over others, we are to be quite assertive in using the gifts of God for our calling as leaders. We can then take criticism without being crushed. We can receive praise without making more of it than it merits. Indeed, such leaders can be humble without humiliation.

Humility and Charisma

Patrick Lencioni, an organizational development writer, speaks of the need for leaders with both humility and charisma. He defines humility as a leader's realization that he or she is inherently no better than the people he or she leads. Charisma is defined as a leader's realization that her or his actions are very important to the success of the organization. Good leaders embrace humility *and* charisma.

Balance is not the answer. Trying to balance the opposing forces by compromising both leads to mediocrity in leadership, says Lencioni. A humble leader must find a way to become more charismatic without sacrificing humility. A charismatic leader must find a way to develop humility without sacrificing the ability to move others.

"The single greatest impediment to raising both ends of the see-saw," Lencioni says, "is the denial that both qualities are important." Humble leaders tend to discount the importance of charisma, thinking it phony. Charismatic leaders rarely discount the importance of humility publicly, but many of them privately believe that humility suggests weakness, says Lencioni.[2]

An Assertive Humility

The humble leader who is also the charismatic leader will understand the lessons Paul taught so long ago. Leaders are carefully humble in keeping themselves and their personal agendas in proper perspective. They do not replace Christ and God's agenda with themselves and their wishes. However, these humble leaders are bold and charismatic, indeed, in keeping before everyone God's vision for humanity and the world.

Humble Christian leaders have a bold message. Leaders witness to God's mighty acts. Jesus said to John's disciples: "Go and tell John what you have seen and heard: the blind receive their sight, the lame walk, the lepers are cleansed, the deaf hear, the dead are raised, the poor have good news brought to them" (Luke 7:22). Rather than call attention to oneself, the leader proclaims what God has done.

Notice the wording that Paul uses: "For the message about the cross is foolishness to those who are perishing, but to us who are being saved it is the power of God" (1 Corinthians 1:18). Our times call for greater assertiveness of what God has done in

Christ. At the same time, there is also a need for greater humility that comes from knowing we are all "being saved."

Humble and assertive leaders often have success and, consequently, face their greatest personal challenge. When the church pews are full, as people become full of God, the blind see, the lame walk, those who hate learn to love, and those who make war come to love peace. Then leaders most need to heed Paul's advice, "Let the one who boasts, boast in the Lord" (1 Corinthians 1:31).

KEEP PERSPECTIVE (TOM)

One of the dangers of leadership is that a role can easily become an identity. Leaders have roles. They are asked to lead a task force, a working group, a committee, a board or council, an organization, or a church. A good leader will be diligent with the assigned responsibility. Problems and conflict occur, however, when the role and the responsibilities become their identity.

The board of trustees of a small church had its own checking account to handle property improvements. The chair treated that checkbook as if it were a sacred object. He and all the trustees created an air of mystery, always being vague about how much money was in the account. They shared little information with the church, even when maintenance issues were discussed. They delayed using the funds, even for obviously needed improvements. They grudgingly completed annual reports.

I once asked the chair why he was so sensitive about the trustee funds. He told me that when he was younger, there was a respected older man in the church who chaired the trustees. This man had found ways to build up a small reserve of funds in case such funds were needed later; some of the reserve came from the chair's own money. As a result, the man guarded each dollar carefully. Before he died, he gave the checkbook to the current trustee chair and asked him to "guard this carefully" and "don't let them waste these funds." The dying man's role had become his identity, and the checkbook became the inheritance he passed on. The new chair was put in the position of holding these funds in trust for someone now dead rather than for the church that was fully alive. All this happened because a past leader lost perspective. He stepped over the line between a role he was to play, and the identity he was to live. Now his successor was following the same misguided path.

When a role becomes an identity, leaders can also feel a false sense of importance. I knew a pastor who looked tired, even haggard, whenever I saw him. We were in a seminar together that met once every few months over a period of time. After the second session he said that he would not be able to complete the experience. As the senior pastor of his church, he explained, there were just too many responsibilities that only he could complete. He said that the distance to the seminar was prohibitive because it was beyond a two-hour drive from his home. He explained that he never took vacations beyond that circumference for fear that someone would become sick or die, and he would not be able to return fast enough. "You have to understand," he said, "in times of emergency, people in my church don't want the associate pastor or a fellow church member. They expect the senior pastor to be there."

I was much younger and less experienced than this man, but I knew enough to understand that he lived in a very small world as a result of turning his role into his identity.

Leaders keep perspective on their tenure and their importance. One of the key ways to keep perspective is to realize that the privilege of leadership is a temporary position. The author of Ecclesiastes captures this: "For everything there is a season, and a time for every matter under heaven" (3:1).

This chapter invites us to gain the perspective that humans are finite, with a limited amount of time and energy to devote even to the best causes and aspects of life. It also helps us understand that we should not confuse our identity as children of God with the gift of leadership in our lives or in the congregations that we lead.

Perspective invites the leader to a posture of humility that is a great advantage to leadership itself. Humble leaders are always looking for the practices and system improvements that will benefit the organization after their tenure is complete. They take a longer view and look for younger or less experienced leaders whom they can mentor into positions of greater responsibility so they can replace themselves when the time comes. They plan for succession not just for their role but also for every role. Rather than mourning the changes that will inevitably come or the false belief that all will be lost when they step out of their role, they focus on leadership development that helps other people grow in their ability to accept future responsibility.

The new chair of a nonprofit board on which I serve started his tenure by creating a list of goals we hoped to accomplish over the next three years. Everyone had the opportunity to offer suggestions. I began to notice that his suggestions always had to do with the long view of the organization's life. He wanted to develop new donors, find new ways to recruit and develop new volunteers, and create a formal process for succession planning of key roles on the board. When I later asked him why these things were so important to him, he said something like, "We're only going to be doing this for a short time, a few years at the most. I want to make sure the important work we are doing is sustained long after we are out of leadership."

Good leaders keep perspective. As a result, they steward their time in ways that advance the good the congregation or organization wants to accomplish.

CHAPTER 6

CULTIVATE LEADERSHIP PRACTICES

DEPEND ON TEAMS

Henry Wadsworth Longfellow wrote his famous "Paul Revere's Ride" in 1860, and it was first published in January 1861. It was this poem that transformed a New England regional folk hero into a national figure of high prominence.

The timing of Longfellow's poem was critical. It was written as the nation moved toward Civil War. And the timing shaped the form of the poem. Longfellow wanted to say to those in the North that one solitary person acting alone could change history.

While the poem was historically inaccurate in virtually all details, according to historian David Hackett Fischer, Longfellow did succeed brilliantly in stamping upon the national memory an indelible image of Paul Revere as a hero, acting as a loner.[1] Longfellow allowed his midnight rider only a single henchman and an anonymous friend. Otherwise, the poet's Paul Revere needed no help from anyone.

What historian Fischer has found is that Revere's accomplishment was much more a group effort. Whereas our image had been one lone person setting out on a solitary mission of warning,

77

Fischer discovered that about sixty people were riding or were otherwise involved. Rather than taking away from Paul Revere's accomplishment, this discovery enhances what he did. Revere was not a lone actor but an organizer, joiner, and motivator—in other words, a leader.

Fischer's research is a good reminder that leadership is always about collective action.

Visions require the work of many people to become reality. Leaders build teams. Much talk of leadership seems to assume a leader working alone, but such leadership is rarely effective. Two significant groups are crucial for leadership effectiveness: those we call "key leaders" and those known as "stakeholders."

Key Leaders. Always be on the lookout for key leaders for the present and for the future. These are individuals without whom the vision cannot be realized. Every church has certain positions of authority and title. One of the most important tasks of a pastor is to discern who will take those positions. Choose well, and you will have a partner in ministry whose wisdom and influence will remove barriers and open a highway for new ideas and initiatives. Choose poorly, and you will find yourself feeling like you are locked in a car with someone who is vying for the steering wheel while you argue about both the destination and which route is best to follow for your journey.

It is critical to take time to cultivate key leaders. The same way that hiring is best done slowly with a number of interviews and reference checks, so we should seek key leaders over time and observe them in a number of settings. Spend time with them in

- social situations, and see how they treat others and whether they tend to emerge as a person to whom others listen and consider a leader.

- small groups or private conversations where they can talk about their faith. Key leaders have to possess spiritual depth and hold a faithful and sound theology if they are to serve the church.

• committees or ministry teams where they lead the group. Here you can observe whether others follow them and if their efforts produce good fruit.

• personal time like breakfast or lunch. Do you enjoy their company? If they are going to be key leaders, you may be spending a lot of time with them, and it is simply more fun to spend time with people you enjoy.

And, finally, observe their habits. Are they as committed with time, talent, and financial resources to the mission of the church as leaders should be?

The total number of key leaders may not be large, but these people are never far from the thinking of the pastor. Future key leaders are often already serving in positions of more limited responsibility. It is helpful to ask in various ministry areas for names of people who have provided great leadership so that you can begin to get to know and observe others you might miss. Then develop relationships. Search for ways to stay in touch, involve, support, encourage, and cultivate—in other words, build the team.

Stakeholders. These are groups whose cooperation is essential. Effective leadership requires the cooperation of most of the people involved in the organization, so paying attention to stakeholder groups becomes very important. In addition to being a group of individuals, the church is also composed of groups with like interests. Their concerns cannot be neglected in pursuit of the vision, no matter how noble the vision is. If their needs and legitimate expectations are overlooked, they can stand in the way of the vision. Good leaders find ways to communicate the vision in a manner that includes everyone and is sensitive to the fact that not all groups in the church will naturally identify with a particular vision. The pastor's careful framing or reframing of the vision can help all experience a sense of connection to it.

It is important to allay their fears. Many stakeholder groups have a long-term presence in the church. Never mind that the members of the "young seekers" class are now all in their seventies. What is important to remember is that many of them originally joined in their twenties and have been together for fifty years. When they hear that change is in the wind, "young" seekers can become fearful or stubborn. If they feel that they are being overlooked or treated as though unimportant, not only will they not participate, but also they may begin to block progress by others. This is why it is so important to communicate the vision and its significance to the congregation. It is important to identify key stakeholder groups and find ways to get their input, seeking their opinion through meetings, surveys, or other means.

Stakeholder groups often have the potential not simply to bless an initiative but to advance the cause far beyond their expectations. A couple in Tom's church offered $10,000 to serve children in Sierra Leone who were victims of child trafficking if people under twenty-five would match their donation. Tom approached a group of high school students at the church, knowing that these students could be key stakeholders in this challenge grant if they could be motivated to serve. A young man from Sierra Leone who had grown up in the center that would benefit from the funds came and spoke to the group. They were so motivated that they began planning fundraising events, selling T-shirts to friends, and inviting their social networks to restaurants that returned some of the profits to their cause. Before long they motivated other stakeholder groups in the church to participate as well. Encouraged by teenagers who were working hard for vulnerable children in another country, the goal was soon met and exceeded, all because several groups were acknowledged as key stakeholders whose potential was taken seriously.

Change is never easy, but it can have surprising and exciting outcomes. Change is possible when leaders see beyond themselves and focus on teamwork.

THINK BEFORE ACTING

It happens so quickly. You see that little envelope symbol on the side of your computer screen. Never mind that you are working on an important project or in the middle of this week's sermon preparation. That little envelope is singing its siren song, calling for you to steer your mouse to its rocky shoals and see what is inside. It looks so inviting. It could be a word of thanks for the insightful words shared at the recent funeral, a note of encouragement from someone who appreciates the time and effort you give each week, or perhaps a willing volunteer offering time and talent to a new ministry. You open the email and find, *Rarely have I been so disappointed by a church leader...*

It is amazing how just a few words can evoke such a powerful response. A few rocks shift deep inside, and suddenly a long dormant volcano becomes active, shooting smoke and hot lava everywhere. Most Christian leaders are by nature and culture deferential and kind people. But when we are provoked, it is tempting for us to tell people *exactly what I have been thinking for a very long time but have been too polite to mention because I am not that kind of a person.*

These situations happen all the time to church leaders. Insults and criticism placed on social media, a smile and handshake in the church atrium that turns into a lecture, or words of frustration about *the direction of the church in recent months* shared in the freezer section of the grocery store while you are standing with a shopping cart and your two children—all are examples of moments when leaders have to be very cautious about their initial responses.

Because these situations are a part of your life, it is important to pause before acting. There is some help in the electronic world. Google added a feature to its Gmail system called "Undo Send" just for such occasions. Originally the sender had five seconds to "undo" the send command. Five seconds seems not very long. In fact, users immediately pressured Google to extend the time to ten, twenty, and eventually thirty seconds. Users pick their own setting.

It turns out that five seconds or less is usually all we need to realize we may have said something we will regret. Unfortunately, when we speak those words, or type them into highly public social media platforms, we do not have an "undo send" button. We live with the consequences, sometimes forever.

Peter Bregman cites a neuroscientist to explain what is going on in our brains when we react in ways we later regret. When something unsettling happens to us, the emotional response center of the brain immediately evokes emotion. That is not bad, except that emotion is not the source of our best decisions. There is something of a battle going on in the brain between the emotional and the more rational. The solution offered by the neuroscientist is, "Take a breath. If you take a breath and delay your action, you give the prefrontal cortex time to control the emotional response." Normally no more than one or two seconds is sufficient.[2]

On a deeper level, there are some things to keep in mind that might create a response regulator that will be helpful everywhere you go.

Realize that for many, church is the great comfort food of life. People often experience hectic, harried, and sometimes dysfunctional lives. When they come to church, they seek that which is familiar and well-known. This is one of the reasons change can be so hard for people in churches and why they can react in ways that seem out of context to their usual patterns and personality. Be aware that the stated concern is just what they are letting you see, and look for ways to minister to what is below the surface.

If these difficult moments are happening on a more regular basis and coming from a number of people, it may be a sign that there are issues that need to be addressed but that people do not understand where the appropriate forum is to address them. Many church leaders offer meetings and surveys where people can share their thoughts and even vent their frustrations in appropriate ways.

Often our reaction to complaints or tension says much about our self-care: rest, time off, exercise, attention to prayer, and the nature of our schedule over the last month. These responses are frequently about *us* rather than the encounter with the person who shared their frustration or the nature of their concern. The best first thought is not, *I'm going to tell this person a thing or two* but, *why am I feeling so angry over what this person has stated?* Understanding the emotional response will often temper our written or verbal response and offer others the benefit of the doubt.

Sometimes it is best to stop the person and offer a second chance for the stating of the concern. The Bible tells us to correct people gently and encourage them in the faith. Sometimes a simple statement is helpful, words like, *I know how much you love Christ and the church. The way you have stated your concern has left me wondering if you know that about me as well. Could you try to share your concern in a way that I might best hear it?*

You have to clean up the mess you create. Emotional responses often create problems far larger and stains far more indelible than the issue first discussed. Save yourself the hassle of all that work. James 1:19-20 (NIV) puts it this way: "My dear brothers and sisters, take note of this: Everyone should be quick to listen, slow to speak and slow to become angry because human anger does not produce the righteousness that God desires."

Whether communicating by e-mail, by text, by telephone, or in person, leaders keep in mind that every word carries with it the potential to build up or tear down, to enhance credibility or damage it. Leaders do not depend on a Gmail tool. They cultivate an internal "undo send" button that they use generously.

FIND A FEW WISE PEOPLE

When pastors tell us about particularly troubling dilemmas they face in their congregations, perhaps the most common advice we offer is, "Find a wise person," or "Find a few wise people." Here is what we mean.

Our experience is that in every church or organization, there are some truly wise people. We are not talking about elderly wise sages, though many will be older folks. We mean, rather, the person or persons with the ability, when approached correctly, to rise above even their own preferences to give good counsel and advice.

Here is an example. You go to the person with a request such as this: "Jane (or John), would you be willing to think with me about something—to be a type of consultant for me for just a moment? I won't quote you, but I need your thoughts." Then you find a nonthreatening way to raise your issue. "Is it just my imagination, or are folks in the Men's Bible Class not staying for worship the way they used to?" Or, "A group of younger people in the congregation wants us to add a new worship service. What are your thoughts about the questions and issues we need to keep in mind if we consider that option? And who else might be involved in the conversation?"

Often such persons will give you their most objective reading of the situation. Or sometimes the wise person will say, "Let me do some listening and get back to you." If you have selected the right persons to consult, even on issues in which they have a stake, they will rise to the occasion and give you their best assessment of reality. Because you have affirmed their fairness and thoughtfulness, they rise to meet your expectations.

Sometimes their wisdom is not about topics related to ministry, but about the network of relationships that compose any organization. Tom's first day at a new church was spent with Gladys, an older member of the church who had lived in the community most of her life. As they drove around visiting elderly members in nursing homes, Gladys told Tom about the church by talking about the people. She knew their interests and their strengths, as well as some of their hardships and suffering. In the years that followed, Gladys became a person who would point Tom in the direction of someone who needed pastoral attention. She also knew which members of the church should be consulted about plans for the future, and who, with a bit of encouragement, might become a new leader. Her relational knowledge often filled in the gaps that a leader new to the congregation experienced. Like an experienced jigsaw puzzle worker, Gladys knew how the pieces of that church could fit together.

These wise ones may or may not hold a formal office, but they are thoughtful and have genuine concern for the best interest of their church and you. Some may be wise about certain topics, yet clueless about others. Think of them as you do that range of mentors from whom you learn. You turn to a particular mentor instead of another based on the situation you are facing. Sometimes you can identify wise people early in your tenure by asking, "Whom should I talk to about this?" You will soon discover if those suggested are objective enough to be contenders for wise people or just people with influence. Wise people usually have influence, but it is their judgment you most need. You may not find a large number of genuinely wise people, but treasure those you find.

Consider categories that might assist you. Some might be organizational: for example, relationships, governance, building issues, insight into the surrounding community, and program development. Others will be spiritual or related to congregational life: small groups, prayer, care of sick people or older adults, concern for the vulnerable, and community outreach. There are people in every church who know about these topics. If you make such a list and find that you have few names from those in the church, consider those to whom you might reach out in the community or in your other networks. These are people to turn to when you are considering the future, or when the unexpected turns up in the present. Their wisdom often arises out of particular interests, vocational experience, or passions they have pursued.

Jim Harnish talks about such people as something of a "tuning fork" for his pastoral leadership. As he puts it, "I knew that when I was in tune with them, I was in harmony with the Spirit's work in the congregation. I knew that they loved me and loved their church enough to search with me for God's best will for all of us."[3]

It is precisely these wise people we most need the longer we are in leadership. Leaders increasingly gain confidence in their own judgments with longevity. They may also be more surrounded by those who share their vision and appreciate their leadership than in earlier years. At such times, these wise spiritual tuning forks, who have a somewhat different range of conversations and experience, become critical for a reality check and sounding board.

ASK THE RIGHT QUESTIONS

Leaders do not need answers.

Leaders must have the right questions.

These two sentences introduce one of the most popular features in each issue of *Leading Ideas*, the online newsletter of the Lewis Center for Church Leadership (www.churchleadership .com) of Wesley Theological Seminary (www.wesleyseminary .edu). This feature grew out of Lovett's realization years ago that leaders spend far too much time trying to figure out the "right answers" to a range of issues facing congregational life while that time would be more profitably used in discerning a few key questions that can change the direction of a church.

Questions are common in the Bible. Jesus was an adept questioner. Today's leaders are so accustomed to providing answers for the questions of others that they often fail to engage the people in identifying and addressing the major strategic challenges in the current chapter of a congregation's life. Since people tend to remember about 20 percent of what they are told but about 80 percent of what they discover for themselves, questions have the beauty of allowing both the issues and the solutions to arise from within the life of a congregation.

There is also great value in having a repertoire of questions that can be used in a range of settings along the path of leadership. Becoming an adept user of questions makes it less likely that your first response to any topic is to state your opinion or "answer." Probing questions honor others and provide additional information for you and those with whom you are engaging. The customary reactions of "I think" or "my take on it is" tend to limit options rather than expand them.

But asking questions is not a delaying tactic or a shrewd way to get more information before giving your view. To use questions in this way quickly reveals a manipulative style and diminishes the leader. Instead, the use of questions is to gather more information in order to clarify for you and others exactly what is at stake.

Leaders have great power, but it is often not the kind of power people assume goes with positions of authority. Few leaders, even at the highest levels of organizations, can—or should—simply decide something and make it happen. This is certainly true for leaders in congregations. God's wisdom is far more abundant than that. However, leaders have tremendous power to set agendas and involve people in reflecting upon topics of concern. Virtually any formal leader can invite those involved in their sphere of leadership into conversations on topics that matter to them and to those with whom they serve.

Leaders do well to frame those topics in clear relationship to the mission of the ministry, either the congregation or one of its specific ministries. More than likely, it is some dimension of that mission that needs special attention. The leader *could* announce that there are problems or opportunities related to this aspect of the mission, but this would position the leader more as an advocate than a leader. There is a time for advocacy, but not most of the time. A more helpful stance is to open subjects for discernment with probing open-ended questions that assume that those engaged are just as committed to a faithful outcome as the leader.

When questioning becomes a way of life for you as a leader, a vast constituency of free "consultants" will enrich your leadership with clues, ideas, patterns, and discoveries well beyond those available to other leaders.

DELEGATE TASKS, NOT RESPONSIBILITY

The ability to delegate tasks while retaining responsibility is critical to fruitful leadership, though it is hard for many pastoral leaders. One reason is that early in our ministries, we are affirmed for what we ourselves do. Often there is no other staff. We do well if we get better at the tasks pastors are expected to do.

Then, we often continue that pattern even as there are more members, staff, and responsibilities. That is when we need to realize that while, in the past, most of what was achieved was from our personal activity, now we will achieve things primarily through the work of others. Our personal work is no less, but the new component is the wide range of ministry of others that needs oversight and direction. Leaders who cannot make this transition will limit their congregations to the amount of work they can achieve by themselves. If one's pastoral identity is that you must know everyone and everything and be involved in virtually all that happens, there will be some fruitfulness, but not much.

Delegation is an art to cultivate but not abuse. Delegation is not dumping a task and walking away. Delegation is more than just assigning work. You maintain a role as leader, but it is no longer to do everything yourself. You continue to give oversight because you cannot shed the ultimate responsibility for the ministry.

There are many benefits to effective delegation. You maximize your time for the tasks only you can do. You can utilize the gifts of those with knowledge you do not have. You help others develop new skills and knowledge. You motivate others as you trust them with important tasks. You increase chances for success through more involvement.

But there are also excuses that may hamper your ability to delegate: You probably can do the task better. You are afraid the other person will fail. You enjoy doing this task. You want it done right away. You think others would want you to do the task. You want to keep your hand in the project.

Some logical tasks to delegate include routine activities, tasks that other team members can do as well if not better than you, tasks that develop the abilities of others and provide a challenge, and projects that are of special interest to others.

There are also tasks *not* to delegate. Most ceremonial events are important for you to do because of your role. You need to take the lead in times of crisis. You will need to take the lead also on policy decisions, many personnel issues, and other matters that include confidentiality considerations.

When there is a gap in the organization, some things will fall on you until there are others with the experience or expertise to do them.

Here are some steps that may help you to delegate appropriately and wisely.

Identify the Task

- Task—make sure it is appropriate for delegating.

- Objective—develop a clear statement of the ultimate goal.

- Assignee—make sure the task fits the person asked.

Communicate

- Describe exactly what you want done, when you want it done, and what end results you expect. Objectives must be specific. Objectives should stretch the individual and offer challenges.

- Explain why the task needs to be done and its importance to the church's mission. Help people put their work in a larger context.

- Discuss the task and objectives, and agree upon realistic and attainable goals and a time frame to use to measure the success of a task's completion.

Ensure Commitment

- Make sure the assignment and objectives are understood and accepted.

Provide Support

- Give the person the authority necessary to complete the task without constant roadblocks or standoffs with others. Link the assignee with the people, money, training, advice, and other resources necessary for the task.

Monitor

- Monitor the progress of the delegation, and make adjustments in response to unforeseen problems. Find the balance between too much attention and too little. Constant interaction gets in the way, but it is only reasonable that there be check-in times to make sure things are on track, to account for new developments, and to make sure the assignee has what is needed. Some keep a "delegation diary" to keep up with assignments so that the assignee and the task are not forgotten. Remember, delegation is not abdication. You are accountable for the success of those to whom you delegate tasks.

Give Credit

- Celebrate and show appreciation when the task is completed. Make sure those whom you asked to do much are appropriately acknowledged and thanked.

When a leader learns the gift and skill of delegating tasks while retaining responsibility, that leader has taken another major step toward strengthening a faithful and fruitful ministry.

CHAPTER 7

KEEP GROWING

KNOW YOURSELF

Leaders can err in two directions. Many begin with themselves as if "I am the beginning point of leadership," to the exclusion of the group and the mission. These leaders are preoccupied with "my values, my ideas, my style." However, some leaders go to the other extreme and seem utterly out of touch with themselves.

Those who become the most effective leaders are persons who understand and accept themselves. They do not operate out of myths of themselves. Nor are they constantly trying to match themselves to the portraits others paint of them. Much of their freedom and power comes from this self-knowledge. People have a right to expect of their leaders maturity that is the product of deliberate introspection and the identification of their particular passions, gifts, and abilities.

Leaders need both self-confidence and an awareness of limitations. Most people believe they know themselves; yet many expend a great deal of energy protecting inaccurate self-images. The solution for this dilemma is both simple and difficult: seek feedback from others, and reflect on what you are doing.

Two practices help in this balancing process: reaching out and withdrawing. First, one must reach out and actively seek feedback. This is often difficult for clergy, many of whom function as the proverbial "lone ranger." Some are in isolated settings, physically separated from colleagues. Others may be isolated by a reticence to confide in others. In order to receive this feedback, pastors not only have to request it, but they must also provide processes to solicit response. They must help their members understand that critique is a valued gift that leads to improvement, rather than an undue criticism that leads to diminished confidence.

Second, one must withdraw to reflect on feedback and use it in self-examination. John Wesley modeled self-examination as a continuing practice essential for the religious leader. In his early years, he set aside time every day for the "examination." Later, he began setting aside each Saturday for self-examination. Finally, in his later years, he developed the habit and inner clock to pause for the first five minutes of each hour to examine the hour past. John Calvin long ago described the need for such self-examination when he said that "without knowledge of self there is no knowledge of God . . . [and] without knowledge of God there is no knowledge of self."[1]

Self-Knowledge in the Service of Leadership

Self-knowledge helps the leader and those whom the leader serves. Robert Greenleaf writes: "Pacing oneself by appropriate withdrawal is one of the best approaches to making optimal use of one's resources. The servant-as-leader must constantly ask: 'How can I use myself to serve best?'"[2]

Leaders constantly experience people relating to them in seemingly strange ways because of their leadership role. Edwin Friedman talks about the need for leaders to practice self-differentiation—staying connected with those they are serving and staying separate enough not to be "swallowed up." Self-knowledge is essential for such self-differentiation.

An Example of Self-Knowledge

A critical dimension of self-knowledge for leaders is to keep things in perspective and not let success go to your head. While a student in New York City, psychiatrist Robert Coles went to see Dorothy Day at the Catholic Worker soup kitchen. He writes of finding Day seated at a table with another woman:

> I found myself increasingly confused by what seemed to be an interminable, essentially absurd exchange taking place between the two middle-aged women. When would it end—the alcoholic ranting and the silent nodding, occasionally interrupted by a brief question, which only served, maddeningly, to wind up the already over talkative one rather than wind her down? Finally, silence fell upon the room. Dorothy Day asked the woman if she would mind an interruption. She got up and came over to me. She said, "Are you waiting to talk with one of us?" One of us: with those three words she had cut through layers of self-importance, a lifetime of bourgeois privilege, and . . . told me . . . what she herself was like.[3]

Mary Catherine Bateson has written about the task each of us has to compose a life. As one grows in knowledge of self and is in tune with oneself, the composing of a life has the character of faithfulness and congruence. Those who are called to be leaders dare not do less.

AVOID COMPLACENCY AND OVERCONFIDENCE (LOVETT)

A few years ago, I was scheduled to preach on the first Sunday of January in a community about two hours from where I lived. When the day of the service came, I got up very early to begin the trip since the weather was not good. I called to make sure the service would still be held. As soon as I started driving, allowing an additional hour to make the trip, I realized that the trip was going to be long and hard.

Snow and ice covered all the highways. There was no other traffic on the roads. Literally, no one! My experience of driving that day went through some very clear and distinct cycles. Later, in reflecting on what happened, I came to see that these are cycles through which we as leaders often go.

Concern and Doubt

At first I wondered if I could make the trip. Could I navigate the slippery highways? Was I adept enough to handle such hazardous driving conditions? Was I up to the challenge? I felt very little confidence in the first part of the journey. I was pleasantly surprised that I could navigate at all, even though I could travel only at a very slow speed. The attention to every detail was not unlike the first few times I ever drove a car. There was no time to think about anything except the next distance ahead.

Competence

After some time facing this driving challenge, I began to figure out some better ways to handle the difficulties I was facing. I learned ways to avoid the worst dangers I faced. I developed techniques that permitted me to drive a bit faster. The fear had not left, but the new confidence meant that my body was not so tense and the chance of finishing the journey successfully seemed much more likely than it had previously.

Confidence

A modest degree of self-confidence came with each mile I successfully completed. Confidence increased as I faced each new challenge and found a way to overcome it. The experience of the morning was giving me confidence that I could figure out how to handle what remained of the trip. It was still taking a long time to cover the miles, but doubts about failure were gone.

Complacency and Overconfidence

The feeling of self-confidence was reassuring. I grew more relaxed. I worried less about the condition of the bridges or the oncoming traffic now developing. I had crossed many bridges successfully and, by now, done well facing increasing traffic, including large trucks.

I began to drive faster. I noticed the road conditions a little less. My sense of competence and confidence were leading me to think less carefully about what I was doing. And then what I had feared all morning happened. A large truck came by, throwing ice and snow over my windshield. I hit a patch of ice, and my car started spinning around and then went off the highway.

Fortunately, no other traffic was coming. I was able to get the car back on the road, and even make my preaching assignment on time, though few others could get to the service due to local road conditions. It turned out that the pastor I called so early that morning, who had assured me that services would be held, had failed to get the weather forecast or look out the window before responding to my question.

All analogies have their limits, but I am struck by the parallels between this trip and the challenges of leadership. The early months and years are filled with concern and doubt because even the best education cannot prepare you for the nonstop first-time challenges you face. As you manage to get through each of those challenges, confidence begins to build. You continue to face new hurdles, but every success makes the next challenge more manageable. Competence leads naturally to confidence. Self-confidence is extremely important to effective leadership. But when confidence morphs into a sense of complacency and overconfidence, danger lurks. We can never rest on our past experience. New challenges require new skills, and many of the new demands may appear without warning as we pay less attention to what is going on around us.

I suspect that all of us will go through this cycle many times as we move to new places of ministry and face challenges we may not have had to address before. And yet, a faithful and fruitful leader will remember what has been learned in the past and will always stay attentive to the new context and the new skills needed to address fresh challenges. A faithful and fruitful pastor will also rest in the confidence that grace has brought us safe thus far, and grace will lead us home.

SEEK AND USE FEEDBACK

Most of us do not enjoy negative feedback even when given with the best of intentions. Tom recalls a time when Sally, a leader in his church, approached him shortly before the worship service.

Sally was preparing the elements for Holy Communion. "May I ask you for a favor?" she said. Thinking she needed me to hand her something, I quickly replied, "Sure. What do you need?"

"When you finish serving communion, could you take an extra minute at the end? As you are placing the bread back on the plate, could you fold the napkin so that its ends are square and place it in such a way that it covers the bread? I noticed the last few times you just sort of tossed the napkins on top like you were finished with lunch. I think you could add to the dignity of the sacrament if you would just take a bit of extra care."

I mumbled a word of appreciation, but I wasn't feeling the love. Who was she to tell me how to handle Holy Communion? I was the ordained one with more than ninety graduate hours in theology. I was not looking for feedback and did not feel that I needed any.

Later that morning as I served the elements to the last members and turned back to the table, I recalled Sally's words. I did what she asked. I placed the bread on the plate. I took the time to fold the napkin properly. I covered the elements carefully. Then I took time to straighten the edge. It was in that moment that I realized two things: Sally was right, and I was better because I acted on her advice.

Some people are critics who seem to have a vested interest in diminishing the people around them. But most people offer us feedback because they care about us and take our work seriously. Leaders learn to assume the best about those who take the risk of saying difficult things, especially when they receive feedback that requires change. Fruitful leaders find ways to solicit the insights and expertise of those around them. They ask others for their estimation about the way they led the meeting or the plans the team agreed to advance. They seek evaluation on small and large things. They are curious about whether their tone of voice was positive or how others may have heard their presentation. While they are confident in their abilities, they are humble enough to hear from others, knowing that improvement is always possible.

One of the keys to hearing feedback is to depersonalize it. When leaders take comments personally, they convert even the most innocent attempt to improve a process into a judgment of their value and worth. In order to hear feedback without a defensive response, keep the focus on the subject at hand. If the person is giving feedback on your leadership at a meeting, ask how you might change the meeting process to enhance the outcomes. If they find your idea confusing, ask them how they might word the concept in a way that would be more understandable. When we can hear that a concept is confusing rather than "you are confusing," we are able to accept the feedback and seek the help of the one courageous enough to bring the problem to light.

Constructive feedback is a sign of love and trust. This is illustrated by another incident when an older member of the church approached Tom just before a funeral. Tom knew her well. She and her husband often helped Tom and his wife by taking care of their young daughters. Tom had no doubt she loved him but was not ready for what he heard as she pulled him aside that day to talk about the deceased.

"You and I both know that she was one of the meanest women who lived in this county. She was mean to her husband, and she said awful things to her daughter, who waited on her for the last ten years of her life. And she was in her right mind when she did it! You don't need to be ugly, but I know preachers like to make it all sound good. But if you start a bunch of flowery comments about her life, I am going to stand up and call you a liar. Now, I believe in you and trust you will do a nice job."

I had two minutes to rethink my remarks, and ended up comparing the deceased to Oscar the Grouch on Sesame Street. Even though she could be abrasive on the outside, her family loved her and her community embraced her and appreciated that she could sometimes share love that her rugged exterior often masked. I do not recall all that I said, but I remember clearly that it was true. It was a celebration more of the care provided by the living than the life of the dead. No one interrupted the service to call me a liar. More importantly, the woman's daughter, who had suffered the slings and arrows of her mother's tongue even as she cared for her, was grateful that I was both honest and uplifting at her mother's funeral. It was the feedback that made all the difference.

While the leader's vantage point enables him or her to see many things about the people led, it is also true that people can see a great deal about the leader as well. To the extent that leaders seek this feedback rather than fearing or resenting it, they will be enriched by the insights and loved for receiving it with humility. It does not take long to separate those who love you and want the best for you from those who simply possess a critical spirit. Actively seek the feedback of those who share your aspirations and hold you in love—and stay open to the possibility that useful feedback can come from other sources as well.

FIND MENTORS (TOM)

I have a dream that I will find the perfect mentor who will not only guide me but also fix me. I would like someone who could help me figure out everything—whom to hire, how to get closer to God, how to set priorities and handle out of control e-mail traffic, how to focus my daily schedule and also make sure I am a great husband and father.

I take some comfort that I am not alone. Most people I know who lead anything appear to have everything under control. Once you know them well enough to get a backstage pass, however, you soon discover that we all have a lot of questions, doubts, and insecurity. Many of us are looking for that charmed person who is a combination coach, mentor, friend, parent, skilled tactician, and fountain of sage advice. Let me save you some time: end the search. That person does not exist. However, that does not mean you are without resources. There are places you can get good advice, insights to your issues, and even answers to your questions.

Read books and let authors mentor you. I have a friend who asks what I am reading every time we get together. He is always looking for authors and titles that others find helpful. Like most leaders I know, he consumes a steady diet of books. Because he spends a good deal of time commuting, he often enjoys audio books and podcasts from a range of people and on a host of topics. I find that books on leadership are helpful, but I also greatly enjoy reading biographies and history. Learning how others met the challenges of their past is a great learning experience that leads me to think creatively about my present.

Reading the original words of great leaders helps me better understand the issues they were addressing as well as how they handled critics who did not share their vision. Following her trip to London, my daughter brought back a book of Winston Churchill's speeches. I am amazed at his mastery of the language and how directly he encouraged a war-weary nation while also confronting those who questioned his judgment as prime minister. Reading again Martin Luther King's words to clergy who wanted him to stay silent instead of protest injustice in his "Letter from the Birmingham Jail" reminded me how easy it is for some church leaders to sit on the sidelines when they should be marching into the fray. These works invite us to reflect on our own life and time with the perspective of a leader history has deemed to be great. The same is true for my devotional and theological reading. Works authored centuries ago often sound as though they were written last week.

You can also find mentors at educational events. I like to travel with others to these events so that we can talk over what the speakers share. Often our conversations will move from the speaker's topic to particular issues one of us is facing. Some of the best mentoring conversations I have enjoyed happened in such settings. It would have been great to have the speaker there with us. However, these friends actually know me and my context well. The questions they ask and observations they share, when connected to the insights of the speaker, may be of greater value than time with the speaker.

Another great source of mentoring is the experts around you. Few people are good at everything. Most of us have a few zones where our competence stands out. I have a friend who is good at investing money. While he would never tell me where to invest, he is happy to give me principles and guidelines to use when considering my financial future. Another friend is an outstanding speaker. When I am having a hard time developing an outline, he knows what questions to ask to prompt my thinking. I have a friend who understands systems and processes. An e-mail or phone call to her will often produce ideas that will benefit my work and make me appear far more capable than I would without her advice. The key is to ask people for specific help in the area that is their sweet spot. There are experts all around you who are more than happy to help you.

There are certified coaches whose training prepares them to be very helpful, especially if you are in a season of discernment about your future. I contracted with a coach for six one-hour sessions. She was immensely helpful at a time when I needed to focus my work and make some difficult decisions about the next season of my life. Let me confess, I am frugal. Some would say cheap. I do not enjoy paying money if I am not sure I will gain something of value. Because I paid this coach, I began every conversation thoroughly prepared. Ahead of time, I sent her a one-page update with suggested topics to discuss so that we would not spend any of the precious time on catching up or small talk. And after the appointment, I got to work on the things we discussed. As a result, I made significant progress on important matters. Sometimes when people say they want a mentor or a coach, what they really want is a shoulder to cry on or a quick fix to a problem. Neither is likely to be very helpful. Hiring a good coach can help because the payment itself will likely be a source of motivation.

Finally, it is important for Christian leaders to remember that they are not alone. We are bold enough to believe that God is with us. As we read the Bible, it becomes clear that God has enjoyed a great number of leadership conversations through the years with a host of leaders. Some were courageous and competent. Others were inept and frightened. Still others were normal people called to do extraordinary things. Talking to God seems to be a make-or-break matter for them. A leader's prayer life can bring clarity to times of confusion and peace to periods of anxiety. Prayer, especially when yoked to honoring the commandment to rest, often opens the gateway of creativity that enables us to envision the future or solve problems in ways we did not previously imagine. It seems trite to say that God is the ultimate mentor, but when we pray sincerely and learn to listen for the prompting of God's Spirit, it is surprising how often we find the answers we are seeking or the people who will be used to bless our efforts.

MAKE SOME DEAR FRIENDS (TOM)

Make friends for yourself. If you are an extrovert, use your natural inclinations to gather some people who can become dear friends. If you are an introvert, as many leaders are, you still need to expend the extra energy required to find dear friends. Fight the instinct to stay alone.

Find people who can become "your people." I do not mean a group of followers or yet another group for you to lead or impress. In fact, that is what you are trying to avoid. These are your people in the sense of your confidants, advisors, and buddies. This is not to say that they will all be just like you or even agree with you. None of us need an echo chamber for our own perspectives. It is even better if they sometimes disagree with you on important matters so that you can have some pebbles in your shoe to annoy you and to remind you that your way of seeing things is not the only way. If they are dear friends, you will think enough of them to listen closely to what they say and consider it carefully. That will expand your thinking and horizons. Pay attention to them not necessarily because they are smarter, but because they are your friends. Leaders need ways to find a different angle on important issues. There is nothing like hearing a contrary opinion from someone you deeply trust.

Maintain old friends if you have them. Old friends have known you for a long time and have the benefit of not being as impressed with your accomplishments as an adult as others may be. They knew you before. They know your stories! The best part of old friends is that, while not as impressed with you as you may be with yourself, they love you anyway. They know you are not all you think you are, and they do not care. You are still important to them. They bring perspective, and leaders need that in regular doses.

If you do not have old friends, it is never too late to make dear friends. These are the people you greatly admire, people you like so much that you keep them on speed dial. You call to encourage them because you believe in them as much as you believe in yourself and maybe even more than you believe in yourself. Dear friends are people you respect and people whose calls you take when you are not taking any calls. They are people who laugh at your jokes one minute and hold you accountable the next. They are people who call the best out of you, who encourage you to think more highly of others than you might otherwise when people have disappointed or hurt you. They tell you to watch how you say things and encourage you to move on. You listen to dear friends in such moments, even as you are ignoring the better angels of your own nature. Deep down, you know they are the kind of people who would throw you a rope if they saw that your swimming had turned to drowning. You trust them more than yourself when life gets turbulent, and that is wise, because they have your interests at heart and the perspective you lack.

Make friends because when you have people in your life who want the best for you and who believe in you, it is a means of grace and a blessing beyond measure. It enables you to feel God's love in a tangible way that even the greatest theologians can only tell us about, not help us experience.

My favorite friendship story in the Bible is the story of Jonathan and David. When they met, Jonathan was the future king of Israel and David was a one-hit wonder (pun intended). As time went by, the two men became dear friends. Jonathan could see the leader David was and the leader David would become. Jonathan was willing to give up his whole future for his friend—to step aside and let David take the crown and the scepter because Jonathan knew David would be better for the nation. Jonathan believed in his friend more than himself, which drove Jonathan's father, the king, crazy. Through the grace of friendship, Jonathan clearly saw all of David's gifts and knew what he must do to protect his friend from his father's paranoia. It is a beautiful story of a man who was dependable, sacrificial, joyful, and courageous. Jonathan believed in David the way God did. He helped David see all he would later become. It's a shame Jonathan died so young, or David might have avoided that whole rooftop liaison with Bathsheba that cast such a pall over the second half of his life. One can just imagine Jonathan on the rooftop, watching David leering at the wife of one of his captains, saying, "Hey pal, you need to get inside and let her have her privacy. I think I hear your wife calling…"

But Jonathan was gone and David never seemed to make another friend like him, which may be why his life got so very complicated. I said the story is one of my favorite friendship stories in the Bible, but the truth is that it is one of the only friendship stories, which may be why, on the whole, leaders in the Bible tended to get it wrong far more than they got it right. It could be that there is some correlation there.

So go make a dear friend. Times will be good, and times will be bad. Friends—real friends, dear friends—who are your people, become the great constant God uses to encourage, cajole, and speak the truth in love into the deepest recesses of our being. They are the messengers God uses to call us to greater things, call us away from destructive patterns, and remind us that we are loved and worthy of love. You may be designed to be a leader, but you are not designed to be a loner. Go make a dear friend.

STAY IN LOVE WITH GOD (TOM)

I have a friend who is a great leader. He is a pastor, and every church he has served has experienced great vitality and has grown in size. People in these churches have told me that they matured in their faith, became more oriented to the service of God, are more generous and joyful, and have been willing to take greater risks, believing that their church was on an important mission. This pastor has habits similar to most good leaders. He reads books on leadership and has studied the practices that lead to greater cohesion and participation in an organization. He takes time to consider what needs to be done in the churches he serves so that they experience progress and momentum in their ministry. He has natural talents and abilities as a leader. All these qualities and many others are good and helpful. But the characteristic that stands out most prominently in his life, the one that everyone readily observes and which has the biggest impact on his leadership, is that after all his years of service, he is still in love with God.

When he talks about the ways God has blessed him and the church he is serving, you have the sense that God is an old friend who stops by from time to time to see how he is doing and to untangle the parts of his life that have gotten too complicated. When he discusses his dreams for the future, it is evident that he is on an adventure, discerning the will of God for his church and then taking steps to live it out, even if the path seems a bit uncertain. His love of God is also evident in his temperament. During good times he is joyful, as though his faith in God has been confirmed through all the good that is happening in the life of the congregation. During more troubled times, he remains calm and steady, certain that God is up to something he does not yet understand but will in time. His trust is in the assurance of God's presence and not in his own ability.

My friend has endured some great tragedies in life that could have caused him to turn his back on his faith in the love and care of God. When disaster struck, he did not feel the compulsion to take on the persona of a rugged leader who was tougher than the hardship he experienced. He was vulnerable and real. He expressed his need for God's love and care. He took time to seek solitude and counsel. Because it was clear that even in tragedy he pursued the fresh wind of God's Spirit, his congregation loved him all the more. They became even more serious about the mission of their church to share the love of Christ with others.

A temptation of Christian leadership is to be so consumed by our service for God that we forget we are servants of God. We forget that God loves us as much as God loves the people we are called to serve or the situations we are called to help transform. Staying in love with God is the way we replenish our life of service and leadership.

In the church I serve, there is a woman who is known for her life of prayer. It is obvious she loves God deeply. She has spent a good deal of time learning to pray and meditate so she can encounter the presence of the divine. Her life is centered more on *being with* God than *doing for* God. As a result, she possesses a calm and deliberate spirit. She has a gentle manner and rarely seems in a hurry or distracted when interacting with others. Like many leaders, my spirituality is often found on the other side of that continuum. Doing for God brings me great joy. It is where

I often feel the presence of the risen Christ. The danger, however, is that it can also lead to weariness and even exhaustion. One day I encountered my prayerful church member in the hallway. She took one look at me and stopped as though alarmed. "Are you all right? You have been too busy lately, haven't you? You need to slow down and get some rest."

She did not mean that I needed more sleep. She meant that I needed to spend some time in God's presence. What concerned me was that she was exactly right. I was amazed at her ability to see this so quickly and discern the cause of my fatigue. The problem was not what I was doing but what I was disregarding. I was not attending to my daily quiet time or to reading the scripture for personal renewal. She knew that I was in danger of *doing* to such an extent that I was neglecting my soul. She also knew that the worst thing that can happen to a Christian leader is to fall out of love with God. Too much doing for God and not enough being with God can soon lead to burn out, or worse. And often what we call "doing for God" is not about God at all. It is about ego or a longing for success that has little to do with God's calling and much to do with personal aspiration.

I once asked my brother if the pastor of his church was a good preacher. He thought about my question for some time and then said, "It depends on what makes a preacher good. He is not a great public speaker. He is not dynamic. He sometimes doesn't have the most interesting illustrations. But he is a good preacher because I am completely confident that he loves God. He is such a fine Christian person that I believe everything he says, and I want to apply it to my life."

Christian leaders who stay in love with God embody something that the world deeply needs. They possess an ethos characterized by love, servanthood, and sacrifice that is distinctive and more important than other skills or insights that leaders acquire. They may not have all the latest leadership techniques, but quite often people will follow them anywhere.

REMEMBER THAT WE ARE WORKING IN SAND

Tom Berlin

Each summer my family spends a week at the beach. And every year my daughters, their friends, and I build a sand castle. This summer it attracted a group of kids who soon took ownership of various parts of the construction process. Eight-year-olds can be tough overseers, wanting sand moved here and there, moats dug deeper or wider, and whole portions of the castle leveled and rebuilt if something looks a bit off. Everyone had ideas, many of which were good, so the building that began in the morning soon extended into the afternoon. They did give us a lunch break, for which I was grateful. By the end of the day, the castle was lovely. A full city with a large citadel in the center, a seahorse medallion on each side, and sea grass flags flying from the towers.

After the pictures were taken, our work was fully admired, and the kids were returned to their cottages, we relaxed. We sat close to the castle, because you have to guard against the random children who do not use their powers for good. The human propensity to destroy is as great as the one to create. We became sentinels. We read our books and napped with one eye open for those who might bring harm to the kingdom.

This is the problem with sand castles. No matter how hard you work, no matter how tall or wide you make them, they are fragile. They are so terribly temporary. They are not built to last. A bit of rain, a barnstorming four-year-old, or heaven help you, high tide, and soon there will be just beach and no trace of the sweat of your brow.

It is important for leaders in the church to understand that we are working in sand. I would prefer concrete. If we were working in concrete, decisions made at a meeting would set and be accepted by everyone. Congregations would not vacillate. Strong programs would remain strong. Meaningful ministries would not suffer from mission creep or the fluctuations that come with the ebb and flow of committed volunteers. Staff members who excel at their work would never take a job elsewhere.

That would be great, but that is not the way ministry works. We work in sand. People come and go; we have to cast vision over and over; we have to raise money again and again. It is important to understand that every aspect of our work requires renewed energy. If we think it is somehow permanent, we will not look as closely. We will make assumptions about the strength of relationships. We will not see the erosive force of weariness or the destructive force of dysfunctional people and the impact these can have on ministry.

The great part of realizing that we are working in sand is that we will not be surprised that we must find new energy to apply to the system to keep the church on track. Understanding the material we are working in helps leaders keep a positive attitude about their work; for they begin the day with the expectation that the work will have to be done and that the work of the leader is never quite finished, even if it can be quite repetitive. As the prayer says, *new every morning is your love, great God of light, / and all day long you are working for good in the world.*[1] The joyful tenacity and persistence reflected in this prayer is the nature of God, and God has created the transient nature of humanity. All of us, it seems, are working in sand.

But underlying all the visions to discern, plans to make, money to raise, leaders to identify, groups to inspire, and human needs to meet, Christian leaders stand on a firm foundation that even the "spiritual forces of evil" (Ephesians 6:12 NIV) cannot dislodge. So let us run the race to which God has called us, knowing that God can take our work in shifting sand and make it be that solid rock on which others can build.

NOTES

1. Build Trust

1. This definition is from Scott Cormode and is the basis for the title of Lovett's book *Take the Next Step: Leading Lasting Change in the Church* (Nashville: Abingdon Press, 2003).

2. Shankar Vedantam, "Lessons in Leadership: It's Not About You. (It's About Them)," *National Public Radio*, November 11, 2013.

3. Robert M. Franklin, *Crisis in the Village: Restoring Hope in African American Communities* (Minneapolis: Fortress Press, 2007), 212–14.

4. Jim Collins, *Good to Great: Why Some Companies Make the Leap...And Others Don't* (New York: HarperBusiness, 2001), ch. 2.

5. This section of the book is an excerpt adapted from Lovett's book *Church Leadership: Vision, Team, Culture, and Integrity*, rev. ed. (Nashville: Abingdon Press, 2010).

2. Lead the Journey

1. Anthony Pappas, *Entering the World of the Small Church*, rev. ed. (Herndon, VA: Alban Institute, 2000), 116.

2. Tom Berlin and Lovett H. Weems Jr., *Bearing Fruit: Ministry with Real Results* (Nashville: Abingdon Press, 2011), ch. 5.

3. "David's Eyes," All Things Considered, *National Public Radio*, June 13, 2000. For more on this theme, see Lovett H. Weems Jr., *Take the Next Step: Leading Lasting Change in the Church* (Nashville: Abingdon Press, 2003), ch. 6.

4. Denham Grierson, *Transforming a People of God* (Melbourne: Joint Board of Christian Education, 1984), 53–60.

3. Set High Standards

1. Emma Coats, "22 #storybasics I've picked up in my time at Pixar," *Story Shots* (blog), accessed April 29, 2014, http://storyshots.tumblr.com /post/25032057278/22-storybasics-ive-picked-up-in-my-time-at-pixar.

4. Communicate, Communicate, Communicate

1. Doris Kearns Goodwin, "Lessons of Presidential Leadership," *Leader to Leader* 9 (Summer 1998): 23–30.

2. Peter M. Senge, "The Practice of Innovation," *Leader to Leader* 9 (Summer 1998): 16–22.

3. LiveScience, "Everyone Thinks They Are Above Average," CBSNews.com, February 7, 2013, accessed February 5, 2014, http://www.cbsnews.com/news/everyone-thinks-they-are-above-average/.

5. Redeem Conflict

1. Joan Chittister, *Wisdom Distilled from the Daily* (San Francisco: Harper San Francisco, 2009), 64–65.

2. Patrick Lencioni, "The Trouble with Humility," The Table Group, accessed February 5, 2014, http://www.tablegroup.com/pat/articles/article/?id=15.

6. Cultivate Leadership Practices

1. David Hackett Fischer, *Paul Revere's Ride* (New York: Oxford University Press, 1994), 332.

2. Peter Bregman, "Undo Send in Real Life," last modified July 15, 2009, accessed February 5, 2014, http://peterbregman.com/articles/undo-send-in-real-life/#.UvJsak0o7IU.

3. James A. Harnish, *You Only Have to Die* (Nashville: Abingdon Press, 2004), 57.

7. Keep Growing

1. John T. McNeill, ed., *Calvin: Institutes of the Christian Religion* (Philadelphia: The Westminster Press, 1960), 1:35, 37.

2. Robert K. Greenleaf, *Servant Leadership: A Journey into the Nature of Legitimate Power and Greatness* (New York: Paulist Press, 1977), 19.

3. Robert Coles, *Dorothy Day: A Radical Devotion* (Cambridge, MA: Da Capo Press, 1987), xviii.

Conclusion: Remember That We Are Working in Sand

1. "An Order for Morning Praise and Prayer," in *The United Methodist Hymnal* (Nashville: The United Methodist Publishing House, 1989), 877.